LINES WEST

LINES WEST

A Pictorial History of the Great Northern Railway Operations and Motive Power from 1887 to 1967

by Charles R. Wood

A MONSTROUS R-2 CLASS 2-8-8-2 with its all weather cab buttoned up tight in the below zero weather exhausts heavily while on the point of a westbound freight. Just west of Minot, on the 3rd subdivision of the Minot Division is Gasman Coulee Bridge, one of the most spectacular structures on the mainline. 1,792 feet long and 117 feet high, it was put into service in 1899, and heavily re-inforced in 1923/24 to handle the bigger power being delivered to the GN. (Casey Adams)

BONANZA BOOKS • NEW YORK

Copyright © MCMLXVII by Superior Publishing Co.
Library of Congress Catalog Card Number: 67-26048
All rights reserved .
This edition is published by Bonanza Books
a division of Crown Publishers, Inc.
by arrangement with Superior Publishing Co.
    d e f g h
Manufactured in the United States of America

Dedication

To the memory of my grandfather, Charles E. Larson, of Minneapolis who surely loved the trains as much as I, and to my wife, Dorothy May, who in the final analysis was the one who was instrumental in putting this book in final form, I dedicate this book.

Charles R. Wood

EMPIRE BUILDER on Stone Arch Bridge
(Great Northern Railway)

Introduction

Lines West is a pictorial history of the east–west mainline of the Great Northern Railway beginning with the purchase of the St. Paul & Pacific in 1878 by James J. Hill and his associates, with emphasis on the diverse and unusual motive power of the road and the geographical settings in which this power operated.

Perhaps more than any other railroad in the country, the Great Northern reflects the driving personality and attitudes of its founder, James J. Hill the Empire Builder, who was well acquainted with and personally guided every aspect of his railroad as it rolled from the beautiful lake country of Northern Minnesota, across the plains and harsh rolling uplands of Central Montana to the evergreen covered slopes of the Cascades, and on to the Pacific Coast.

Most northerly of all our transcontinental railroads, the Great Northern was one of the few to be built without the aid of generous land grant to finance its push west out of the Dakotas to Puget Sound, although a land grant did make it possible for the immediate predecessor of the Great Northern (The St. Paul, Minneapolis & Manitoba) to start its corporate life with money in the bank and sound credit.

For nearly thirty five years after the completion of the mainline in 1893, the road was still plagued with the operating hazards and bottleneck that existed over the mainline through Wellington, and it was only upon completion of the 8 mile Cascade Tunnel in 1929, that the Great Northern achieved the finest mainline profile of any of the northwest transcontinentals.

The electrics of the Great Northern, operating as they did over a sub-division high in the rugged and forbidding North Cascades, largely removed from the sight of travellers, did not receive the exposure and publicity that the electrics of other railroads such as the Pennsylvania or Milwaukee did, and yet without them it is inconceivable that the Great Northern would have ever built the longest tunnel in the western hemisphere.

Most of the photos of the steam power, and the trains they pulled were taken within the decades from 1930 to 1950 when steam was at its peak, an era within the memory of most readers. Perhaps the photographs in this book will recall vividly for many, the time when steam power dominated the railroads of this country.

Little attempt has been made to give a complete chronological sequence to the diesel power of the Great Northern, because most diesels within a model classification. differ only in detail, regardless of whether they were built in 1939 or 1951. Instead, a selection of photos of diesels in action on various parts of the Great Northern that illustrate settings descriptive of the country the GN serves, was chosen.

From the era of steam power to the day of the modern diesel, the history of the GN has been one of constant change and progression. Now in 1967, the motive power and equipment of the Great Northern emerges with a new look. Rocky, the GN trademark, has been modernized with a huskier, more youthful and virile image, and the familiar Omaha orange and Pullman green has given way to a new corporate color, "Big Sky Blue," named after the "Big Sky Country" of Minnesota, The Dakotas, Montana, Idaho, Washington and Oregon.

Charles R. Wood

AN EASTBOUND DRAG behind a roaring 2-8-8-2 comes around a sharp curve heading upgrade towards Skykomish. The 1% ruling grade to "Sky" isn't overly difficult up through Sultan, Goldbar, Index and Grotto as the railroad climbs out of the Snohomish River Valley and into the Cascades, but in the east end of the yards at Skykomish the stiff 2.2% grade begins and continues to Scenic 18 miles away at the west portal of Cascade Tunnel. The big electric motors take over at Skykomish humming and growling every foot of the way to the tunnel as the drag of thousands of tons in the cars pulls back with a nearly equal force. (Stuart B. Hertz)

7

Acknowledgments

Many and varied sources were explored in the search for material for this book and for their generosity, assistance and encouragement the author most gratefully acknowledges the help of the following people:

John Miller, Jim Frederickson, Ken Usher, R. G. Johnson, Fred Jukes, Stan Gray, Fred Forester, Wally Swanson, Mike McLaughlin, Paul Coffin, Joe Gibson, Eva Anderson, The *Wenatchee Daily World,* The *Everett Herald*, Montana Historical Society, Seattle Public Library, Washington Historical Society, John Labbe, Officers and Past Officers of the Pacific Northwest Region of the National Model Railroad Association; Howard Durfy, President, Phil Kohl and the late Walt Mendenhall.

A special word of appreciation is due the photographers who contributed to this book and without whose generous contribution this book would not have been possible. Dr. Phil Hastings—widely recognized as one of the leading railroad photographers, Phil Kohl—photographer, perfectionist and master of darkroom technique, Casey Adams—historian, photographer and collector who made the steam section of this book possible, Stuart Hertz—newspaper photographer with an artist's touch, W. R. McGee—NP conductor and expert photographer, Walt Thayer—photographer and collector of railroad memorabilia, Claude Witt—GN conductor, photographer and collector of GN memorabilia, Mrs. Lucille Mason—professional photographer and artist who pulled prints out of nearly impossible old negatives, and to Mrs. Lee Pickett who generously permitted a search of her late husband's photographs of the building of Cascade Tunnel.

The reader will recognize too that the Great Northern Railway made a significant contribution to this book through the offices of the Public Relations and the Engineering Departments. Without the assistance of these departments much of the rare material that is incorporated in this book would not have appeared. Mr. Frank Perrin and Ken Foreman of Public Relations, Chuck Nelson, Walt Grecula, Max Rader and T. C. Nordquist of the Engineering Department. Gentlemen, to all of you—thank you!

If through some mischance an acknowledgment was inadvertently left out of this compilation the author trusts it will be found in its appropriate place on the pages that follow.

1895

1914

1921

1922
to
1935

1936

1967

CONTENTS

(Phil Kohl)

JAMES J. HILL
The Empire Builder

THE EARLY DAYS

The story of the Great Northern Railway is the story of James J. Hill an able, powerful, and shrewd man who was to become known as The Empire Builder. Hill, a Canadian by birth, came to St. Paul, Minnesota in 1856 at the age of 18, and within ten years was the most successful forwarding agent in St. Paul. He started a steamboat business on the Red River of the North carrying settlers and supplies between Fort Ambercrombie on the American side to Fort Garry (Winnipeg) on the Canadian side that challenged the steamboat monopoly of the powerful Hudson's Bay Company. Hill ostensibly sold his equipment and entire business to Norman W. Kittson (formerly Hudson's Bay agent in St. Paul) who formed the Red River Transportation Company of St. Paul, but actually remained as a secret partner and thus established the basis of his fortune. From 1866 to 1878 Hill also acted as an agent for the First Division of the struggling St. Paul & Pacific, and during this period realized that in time, with proper management, the railroads would dominate traffic in the Northwest. In 1878 Hill joined with Kittson, Donald A. Smith (Canadian Resident Governor of Hudson's Bay Company), and George Stephen (President of the Bank of Montreal) to purchase the properties of the bankrupt and incomplete St. Paul & Pacific for around $9,000,000. Hill and his associates intended to complete the road from St. Paul to St. Vincent at the Canadian border to meet the branch of the CPR being constructed from Winnipeg, Manitoba south to the border. Since the CPR was not complete from east to west, everything moving into Winnipeg by rail had to be funneled through the Northwest gateway of Minneapolis/St. Paul, and this line from St. Paul to Canada presented possibilities of a very profitable business supplying Manitoba and all the Northwest Territories.

The St. Paul & Pacific through its predecessors had been granted, by acts of Congress in 1857, 1865 and 1871, lands totalling 2,811,142 acres if the railroad could meet the terms of its charter and be completed by January of 1879. In January of 1879 the St. Paul & Pacific was completed by Hill, the terms of the charter were certified, and the land

grand award was made. In May of 1879 Hill and associates organized a new corporation, the St. Paul, Minneapolis & Manitoba, to take over the properties of the St. Paul & Pacific, and sold 2,713,399 acres of the land awarded to its predecessor for $15,880,595, putting the new Manitoba on a firm financial footing—unlike many railroads in this free wheeling era.

With the organizing of the St. Paul Minneapolis & Manitoba in 1879 Hill set about to consolidate and expand his gains in Minnesota, and also push the legislature of the Dakota territory for a charter to build on the west side of the fertile and booming Red River Valley in what is now North Dakota. Hill had his charter in 1880 and began laying track on the west side of the Red River around Grand Forks, North Dakota. The purpose seemed to be to continue to expand and consolidate the position of the railroad in the Red River Valley. However, the vast distances of the West reaching beyond must have beckoned to Hill much as the possibilities of the Canadian business did just a few short years before.

He watched and waited (with some disapproval) as the Northern Pacific was being completed further to the south. He thought it poorly located, and failing in many areas, to take advantage of the terrain, resulting in excessive construction costs. The Northern Pacific was deeply in debt and would soon face a receivership due to its rapid expansion, and costly mainline construction without sufficient branches to serve as profitable feeders to the mainline.

While the NP rushed pell mell from Duluth to Tacoma, the Manitoba was making haste slowly During this period from 1880 to 1883, Hill gained access to the Great Lakes at Duluth, was active through his agents in colonizing Northern Minnesota and Manitoba, organized the Minnesota Transfer Company where all roads coming into Minneapolis/St. Paul could interchange freight equipment, and in 1886 gained permanent access to Chicago through the Chicago, Burlington & Quincy railroad. In retrospect, if Hill had had the sumptuous land grant from the Dakotas to the Pacific that the Northern Pacific had during its building, perhaps the Manitoba too would have made a headlong rush for the Pacific Northwest. Without such a grant, the Manitoba busied itself under Hill, in making itself so strong in Minnesota and North Dakota, that when the time did come to push first into Montana and then across the Rockies and Cascades, it was able to do so without bleeding itself white.

In 1886 the tip off to the push west came when the Manitoba, after constructing only a relatively few miles of track per year in North Dakota, suddently punched almost 122 miles west to Minot, and constructed another 100 miles of track elsewhere in North Dakota. This type of fast construction was typical of Hill only when a distant goal was in sight. That goal was Great Falls, Montana nearly 600 miles to the west, and again characteristic of Hill, the goal was not strange country without friends or connections. These friends had organized in 1886, the Montana Central railroad which was to connect the territorial capital at Helena with the new city planned at the Great Falls of the Missouri where Lewis and Clark in their explorations of 1804/06 had had so much difficulty.

Construction of the Manitoba west from Minot began in April of 1887 with nearly 10,000 men employed as locating engineers, bridge and building gangs, grading crews and track layers. The prime contractor Shepard-Winston and Company had worked previously for Hill when he had sent them north with Van Horne of the Canadian Pacific. A tremendous camp sprang up at the railhead, just outside of Minot, and through the spring of 1887 the facilities of the railroad were fully engaged in hauling rail, timbers, ties, grading equipment and all the supplies necessary to build a railroad. Out on the prairie to the west of Minot, the railroad progressed at the rate of better than 3¼ miles per day during May, June, July and August, and by the middle of October the rails were being spiked down at Sun River, Montana, nearly 550 miles from Minot. Here the Manitoba connected with the rails of the Montana Central, which during the same period had completed its part of the line between Sun River, Great Falls and Helena—a distance of 95.8 miles. In just 7½ months 643 miles of continuous railroad had been constructed, and the Montana Central continued construction during 1888 to reach Butte where the Manitoba could interchange freight and passengers with the Union Pacific for points in Oregon and California.

Meanwhile, back in Minnesota, Hill had organized the Eastern Minnesota railway for a direct connection with Duluth and Superior, Wisconsin, and now had connections between the major cities of Minnesota, the Great Lakes and the new railroad in the west. In addition Hill organized the Northern

Steamship Company to carry wheat on the Great Lakes and put six new modern steamships in service.

With events moving well for the Manitoba in Minnesota, North Dakota and Montana, with profits already rolling in from the grain elevators in Duluth, with wheat moving out of areas served by the Manitoba, with coal from Montana mines moving to the Great Lakes behind Manitoba motive power on Manitoba rails, James J. Hill turned his attention to the west that still stretched nearly 1,000 miles beyond the tracks at Pacific Junction a few miles west of Havre. He organized the Great Northern Railway Company around the charter of the old Minneapolis & St. Cloud Railroad Company in September of 1889, and the Great Northern then leased the Manitoba for 999 years. This lease stayed in effect until November 1, 1907 when the GN officially purchased the St. Paul, Minneapolis & Manitoba along with the Montana Central, Seattle & Montana, and many other subsidiary companies. In 1890, shortly after the incorporation of the Great Northern Railway, the directors of the Great Northern requested Hill "to extend its lines westward from some suitable point in Montana to Puget Sound."

Preliminary location work west of Havre had been underway since the Spring of 1889. There were two known passes south of Great Falls, but either of these meant a longer mainline (by over 100 miles) to the coast. There was also Cut Bank Pass located further north in what is today Glacier National Park, but the summit of this pass was over 7,500' high. Hill wanted a pass that would slide across the backbone of the Continental Divide at an elevation that would permit a low ruling grade, eliminating or at least minimizing helper districts, for he knew that low rates, profits, and dividends were not based on doubleheading tough mountain grades.

Earlier explorers and engineers including Merriwether Lewis, Isaac Stevens and A. W. Tinkham had looked for, but never found a hidden pass, which according to Indian legend lay close to the headwaters of the Marias River. Such a pass, if it existed, would permit an almost direct line west from Havre to Kootenai River Valley, already chosen as the route through western Montana and into Idaho.

In December 1889 John F. Stevens, only 36 years old, but one of the finest locating engineers in the country (he had among many other accomplishments helped locate the Canadian Pacific mainline through the formidable Canadian Rockies) accompanied by a Flathead Indian guide from the Blackfoot Agency, ranged north and south of today's mainline in search of the hidden pass. Perhaps the Indians actually knew the general location of this pass, but tribal superstitions concerning an evil spirit that inhabited the pass prevented the effective exploration of the area and resulted in days of fruitless searching. On the night of December 11th, following a branch of the Marias River, John F. Stevens walked into the hidden pass alone, proceeding far enough to the west to make certain he had actually found it—then spent the rest of the night tramping through the snow in below zero weather to keep from freezing to death.

Stevens had found the lowest crossing of the Rocky Mountains, and the railroad could build through the pass without the need for a summit tunnel. He had shortened the mainline to the coast by 150 miles with a ruling grade of only 1% westbound and a moderate 1.8% eastbound. Finding this pass was to pay handsome dividends to the stockholders of the Great Northern for years to come. Once over the summit and through the pass the mainline slipped easily down along the middle fork of the

Flathead River to Columbia Falls and then on to Whitefish. Here it turned northwesterly along the water level grade of the Kootenai River to Bonners Ferry, and then southwest along the Pend d'Oreille and Little Spokane Rivers to Spokane, Washington the capital of the "Inland Empire."

At Spokane in 1892, Hill was ahead of his tracks as usual, while Stevens was busy surveying and locating in the Cascades. At a memorable meeting with the citizens of Spokane, Hill cleared the way for the coming tracklayers by generously accepting the offer of Spokane to donate a right of way through the city to the GN. Hill had pointed out an alternate route open to the railroad that bypassed Spokane far to the north, and the alarmed citizenry who had assumed that the GN would go through Spokane in any event and by competition, relieve the onerous rates of the NP, hastened to grant the right of way.

Now the railroad continued through the rich wheat country of Eastern Washington across the mighty Columbia River, through Wenatchee on the

ONE OF THE RAREST PHOTOS in this book is reproduced showing the William Crooks at Elk River, Minnesota in 1864. At the time it belonged to the First Division of the St. Paul & Pacific Railroad a predecessor of the Great Northern. The Wm. Crooks was the first locomotive in Minnesota and adjacent territory. Built by Smith & Jackson at Patterson, N.J. the little 4-4-0 was brought to St. Paul in 1861 on a Mississippi River steamboat, and named for the Chief Engineer of the St. Paul & Pacific Railroad, Colonel William Crooks. (Great Northern Railway)

opposite bank, and up again along the Wenatchee River through the Tumwater Canyon into the foothills of the Cascades. Here among the rugged peaks of the North Cascades the railroad ran into real trouble. With the goal of Puget Sound almost in sight, with barely 100 miles to go into Seattle, the GN was faced with vertical escarpments at around 3,400' elevation that even the fine locating engineer John F. Stevens was unable to get the railroad through without resorting to a 2½ mile long tunnel. A tunnel, however, would require years to build and the railroad had to be completed now. The only possible solution was to resort to a series of switchbacks—four on the east side and five on the west side of the summit—to lift the railroad up to and across the summit and down the other side. These switchbacks hampered the operation of the road for seven years until the old Cascade Tunnel was opened in 1900, but the road was completed in 1893, on schedule, with the last spike hammered down near Scenic, Washington in January, and transcontinental service to Seattle over the rails of the Seattle & Montana from Everett started in mid-summer.

Unfortunately, the opening of the Cascade Tunnel in 1900 did not bring an end to the troubles of the road in the Cascades. No one could have foretold accurately the effect on railroad operation of millions of tons of snow accumulated on the high parapets of the Cascades all the way from the steep Tumwater Canyon, just west of the old Division point at Leavenworth, to the lower valley of the Tye River on the west side near Scenic (then called Madison). This stretch of track most of it on a tough 2.2% grade, wound, curled and spiralled a distance of over 40 miles up to Wellington at the west entrance of Cascade Tunnel, and then wound down again to finally reach the easier grade along the Wenatchee River.

All of this line was exposed to avalanches and slides, and for many miles near Wellington the mainline clung to the precipitous mountainsides by

its fingertips. In this area the mountain hoggers rode with eyes alternately on the roadbed and on the slopes, rising perpendicularly from the wheel journals on the near side and falling steeply away on the opposite side. The ears were tuned for the low rumble that signalled an avalanche, while a sixth sense often saved a train and crew from impending disaster. Such hazards in the wintertime made the GN operation across Stevens Pass as tough as any operation faced by either a standard or narrow gauge road anywhere in the country.

To partially alleviate these difficulties the railroad built a series of immense snowsheds from Scenic to the west entrance of the small yard at Wellington. These huge snowsheds were reinforced, rebuilt and extended practically every year from the time the road opened in 1893 until the old line was abandoned in January 1929. For over thirty-five years the road invested fortunes in construction and maintenance of these sheds and saw equally large sums disappear in the form of sticky white snow thrown over the banks by whirling rotary blades. In 1925 the situation was finally resolved when the Directors of the Great Northern, after considering many engineering studies and proposals, authorized the building of the eight mile long new Cascade Tunnel, a new line through Chumstick Canyon, and electrification of the sub-division between Skykomish and Wenatchee.

James J. Hill did not live to see the start of the new tunnel in the Cascades—he died in St. Paul in 1916—but he had forecast just such a tunnel. On his last trip over the entire line in 1914, he had told Ralph Budd then President of the GN, "Some of you will live to see this mountain line eliminated." With the completion of the Cascade Tunnel the Great Northern achieved—as Jim Hill had visualized it long ago when the Pacific extension of the Great Northern started at Pacific Junction, Montana —the best profile and mainline of any railroad serving the Pacific Northwest.

THE WEST ENTRANCE to Horseshoe tunnel, along the old mainline to Wellington, reposes in dark and brooding silence in 1964. Constructed in 1893, and used until 1929, the almost circular tunnel still smells faintly of coal smoke and engine oil. (H. A. Durfy)

A HUGE STEEL REINFORCED WOODEN PLOW mounted on the lead engine of a double headed passenger train battles the snow in Minnesota in the late 1870's. The brace of American types, similar to the Wm. Crooks, have their work cut out for them as do the crew and section men. When snow too deep or too compacted to be readily pushed off the track was encountered, the engines would back up for a distance, come to a halt, and then with the throttles opened would charge at the mass of snow intending to break it up and push it aside by sheer force. One of three things happened when the plow hit the snow: either the engines broke through and continued on their way; or the snow gave a little and then as further resistance was encountered the engines stopped—probably stuck fast; or the lead engine derailed from snow and ice forced under the plow, and the second engine still pushing jammed into the first. Plowing and bucking snow was a job dreaded by enginemen, tough hard dangerous work, complicated by the icy winds that swept across the Northern Plains. (Great Northern Railway)

15

THE CURVED STONE ARCH BRIDGE, built across the Mississippi River between St. Paul and Minneapolis during 1882/83 by the Minneapolis Union Railway Company, a belt line owned by the St. Paul, Minneapolis & Manitoba, was one of the most difficult and costly undertakings ever made by James J. Hill. Nineteen months in the building, and at a cost of $650,000, the 2,100′ bridge with graceful stone arches made of St. Cloud granite angles across the Mississippi River below St. Anthony Falls. It is the only structure on the Great Northern that James J. Hill allowed to be named after himself, and his name and that of Colonel C. C. Smith, the Chief Engineer of the Great Northern, are inscribed in the cornerstone. Hill built for the future, and the bridge which still is in use today is a monument to his judgment and railroad building philosophy. (Great Northern Railway)

16

SHOWN IN THIS PHOTO from the 1890's is the original timber trestle over Gasman Coulee built by the St. Paul, Minneapolis & Manitoba in 1886/87. Gasman Coulee, about three miles west of Minot was the point, from which the westward extension of the Manitoba began, on April 2, 1887, with 3,000' of track laid the first day. The trestle containing nearly a million and a half board feet of timber was partially destroyed by a heavy windstorm on August 14, 1898 and trains detoured on a temporary track, one and a half miles long down in the Coulee until January of 1899 when a new steel bridge was completed. (Great Northern Railway)

OUT ON THE SEEMINGLY LIMITLESS PRAIRIE west of Minot, North Dakota in 1887 track laying teams spiked down the rails of the Manitoba. Material trains brought the rails, ties and other supplies to within a half mile of the rail head and iron cars, drawn by horses, moved the rails to the end of track, while teams went ahead with ties and timbers for bridges. By such methods a surprising amount of distance could be covered. On one day, August 11, 1887, 44,100' or a little more than 8⅓ miles of track were laid—a world's record. (Great Northern Railway)

MEN IN SEARCH OF ADVENTURE, men down on their luck, drifters, gamblers, homesteaders, immigrants, boomers, red men and white labored side by side in the Montana Territory punching the rails of the St. Paul, Minneapolis and Manitoba across the bleak northern prairies, in 1887. The smoke of little 4-4-0's columned into the sky over the land where only a few years before the Indians had hunted buffalo, and the whistles of the trains called across the prairie that once had echoed only the cry of the wolf. The homesteaders would follow soon in their zulu cars, for the westward expansion of the Great Northern was in full swing, and within a decade the territories of Dakota, Montana, Idaho and Washington would be admitted to the Union. (Great Northern Railway)

BRONZE STATUE OF JOHN F. STEVENS, by the famed sculptor Cecere, was erected by the grateful Great Northern in 1925 close by the mainline in Marias Pass at almost the exact spot where Stevens had tramped through the snow on the night of December 11, 1889 after finding the long hidden pass. Stevens later became Chief Engineer of the Great Northern and also located the new 8 mile long Cascade Tunnel, completed in 1929. (Great Northern Railway)

IN 1892, during the building of the Pacific extension of the Great Northern, Two Medicine bridge, located just east of the summit of Marias Pass, is still under construction. During the ten years the 214' high wooden structure was in use it was highly respected by GN enginemen. In windy weather the bridge swayed noticeably with timbers creaking and groaning and the dispatcher would close the structure until the wind subsided. In 1900 a new steel bridge, close by the original location, replaced the fragile wooden structure. (Great Northern Railway)

THE OFFICE CAR of Shepard-Winston & Company, the prime contractors on the 1887 extension of the St. Paul, Minneapolis & Manitoba from Minot to Great Falls, is pictured near Fort Assiniboine, Montana Territory on September 14, 1887. (Montana Historical Society)

GN PASSENGER TRAIN ENGINE No. 2 south of Bellingham, Washington in the late 1890's has only recently become a Great Northern engine. The engine is an ex-Fairhaven & Southern 4-6-0 from a Bellingham railroad that passed into the hands of James J. Hill in 1890 connecting with another Hill subsidiary, the Seattle & Montana Railroad, at Burlington, Washington in 1891, to complete the Shore Route between Seattle and Bellingham. With the acquisition in 1890 of the New Westminster & Southern, Jim Hill had his connection into Vancouver, B.C. through the Canadian Pacific at New Westminster B.C. For a time all of these smaller roads, purchased or controlled by the GN, operated under their own names, but by the turn of the century, the Great Northern name appeared north and south of Seattle as well as on the mainline to the east. (Fred Jukes courtesy Great Northern Railway)

PASS ISSUED by the Great Northern Express Company, a wholly owned subsidiary of the Great Northern Railway. (H. A. Durfy)

PRIOR TO 1906, when King Street Station was completed, the Great Northern station was located between Marion and Columbia streets along the waterfront on—aptly named—Railroad Avenue. Largely at the insistence of James J. Hill, who realized that this fine deep water frontage would always be constricted by the terminal and yards of the railroad in this location, the railroad terminal was moved away from the waterfront, further south, about a mile beyond the main business section of Seattle. Today a few of the buildings visible in this 1896 photo still remain, including the tall steam power plant smokestack. The mainline tracks are now in a two track tunnel running generally under 4th Avenue, and almost directly over the old track location there is a tremendous double deck highway viaduct running along the length of the waterfront, while parallel switching leads below serve the docks and warehouses. (Great Northern Railway)

ENGINE NO. 224 with a southbound passenger train at Bellingham, Washington about 1904, like much of the power used on the Seattle to Vancouver, B.C. run in the early 1900's, was not typical of GN locomotives used elsewhere. Many of these engines came to the GN when railroads were purchased and all of their equipment and facilities were turned over to the Great Northern. No. 224 was primarily assigned to passenger service as evidenced by the semi-retractable front coupler and lack of steps on the pilot or pilot beam for the convenience of switchmen.

Heavy, unwieldy and great finger mashers, retracting type couplers were a source of annoyance to all concerned, but were of some value in preventing wagons or carts from becoming impaled upon them when grade crossing collisions did occur. Briefly in vogue early in the century, they disappeared for many years, to reappear again in the 1930's on the Union Pacific, New York Central and a few other roads on high speed passenger or freight engines. (Fred Jukes courtesy Great Northern Railway)

THE FIRST STATION at Madison (later Scenic) perches high above the rails on the mountainside. Further downgrade the watertank has been built directly beside the tracks to service the eastbound trains that come slogging up the long grade from Skykomish. The passing of a train, in this remote location in the late 1890's, was an occasion for the operator and his family serving as their only communication with the outside world other than the slender fragile threads of the telegraph wire. In the winter, the passing of a train could be delayed for many hours by trouble "up on the hill" and the telegraph, too, was frequently taken out of service by the snow and falling snags. (Claude Witt)

ENGINE NO. 1000, one of the early ten wheelers, is spotted with her crew near the station at Wellington around the turn of the century. Quarters for the many employees who were stationed at Wellington may be seen on the high bank behind the engine. The white scar seen above the roof of the station is one of the cuts along a switchback on the side of the mountain. (Claude Witt)

LEGS 1, 2, 3, AND 4 of the switchbacks above Wellington are visible in this photo taken by Harrison Usher not long after the Cascade Tunnel was opened in 1900 and the switchback route abandoned. The distance between Wellington and Cascade Tunnel Station is less than three miles as the crow flies but by the switchback route it was roughly nine miles. The grade was a forbidding 4% with the switchbacks in some areas literally pinned to the sides of the mountains and crews were specially trained to handle trains across them. Going up was bad enough as the train sawed back and forth ever higher, but coming down was even more hazardous, as the train constantly tried to break the restraining grip of the primitive air brakes.

Further complicate this operation with immense drifts of soggy snow slid across the right of way or compacted into icy masses, run engines short on coal and water, shatter rotary plow blades with rock and timber buried in the slides, and train operation became a slow, grinding, dangerous and exhausting experience that could take hours or even days to cover a few miles. (Harrison Usher)

IN THIS EARLY 1900 SCENE, twelve wheeler No. 709 stubbed its pilot on a snowslide right in Wellington yard and derailed across a yard switch. Fortunately, the accumulated snow on the ledge of ground beside the tracks has prevented the engine and tank from turning over and section men with timbers, heavy jacks, block and tackle are preparing to lift the engine upright and move it sideways to where it can be re-railed. (Harrison Usher)

A ROTARY is in action in the yards at Wellington after a heavy snowfall in the spring of 1906. The small yard was plowed continually during the winter months to keep the tracks open, and surprisingly the snow problem was worse in the Wellington yards than just 3 miles away at Cascade Tunnel Station—on the east side of the summit. (Harrison Usher)

THE STATION AT WELLINGTON is shown in this photograph taken in the early 1900's by Mr. Harrison Usher a telegrapher on the GN and assigned to Wellington. Wellington had just one reason for its existence—the railroad. Located high in the Cascade mountains and removed from contact with the rest of world except by railroad it was a remote yet busy spot the year around with all the traffic moving east and west funneled through its small yards. After the disaster of 1910 the railroad changed the name of the town to Tye and rebuilt all of the facilities that had been wiped out by the avalanche.

The quarters behind the station were relatively deserted during the summer months, but during the winter, were filled to capacity with rotary plow crews, helper engine crews, extra section men, operating personnel, and a multitude of specialists whose jobs were maintaining, operating and supervising one of the toughest operating districts to be found in the U.S. and Canada. Twelve and sixteen hour days for the crews and operating personnel were standard procedure and twenty four hour days were not uncommon when the line was blocked by snow and slides. (Harrison Usher)

A RAILROAD SECTION CAR is being used as transportation for one of the telegraphers and his family from their quarters at Wellington to some point down grade—possibly the spa at Scenic Hot Springs. The derby hats worn by the two boys emulated the headgear of the train crews, for the derby, not the wide brimmed Stetson of western fame, was the choice of railroad men in the late 1880's and early 1900's. The derby was more practical, when leaning out of a narrow cab or vestibule window and remained much more firmly on the owner's head in the passing breeze. (Harrison Usher)

ENTERTAINMENT AT WELLINGTON during off duty hours was largely a matter of providing your own or doing without. Harrison Usher, smoking a pipe and playing a guitar, is joined by three other off duty GN employees for companionship and music. Many men were musicians—of a sort—and simple pleasures like this, long before the days of radio and TV served to make the long evenings more enjoyable. (Harrison Usher)

A ROTARY PLOW is moving slowly up the safety track beyond the station at Wellington in the early 1900's plowing out the accumulated snow. As a precaution, another rotary facing in the opposite direction, is coupled to the pusher engine so that the entire outfit will not be stuck if the disturbed snow starts to slide across the track. Westbound trains, coming downgrade, had to signal the operator at Wellington station that they were under control before the switch leading into the safety track would be lined for the main. The safety track was used, on occasion, by trains out of control, and if the speed was not too excessive, momentum would be lost on its steep incline. (Harrison Usher)

A WESTBOUND FREIGHT slowly moves towards the east portal of the old Cascade Tunnel in 1905 as the fireman, leaning far out of the cab window to watch the photographer, discovers "two knights of the open road" enjoying a free ride on the pilot of the engine. Free loading passengers, familiar with the almost suffocating gas and smoke conditions in the tunnel, would unload from their perches on the car tops or ends at Cascade Tunnel Station or Wellington. and look for an open boxcar or for the most smoke free spot of all—the engine pilot just out of sight of the busy crew. (Harrison Usher)

THE ORIENTAL LIMITED, train #1 west-bound, pounds along the Wenatchee River west of Leavenworth in the Tumwater Canyon climbing the east side of Stevens Pass, during the early summer of 1909. Doubleheaded be-cause of the 2% grades not far from this spot, the Consolidation on the point serves as helper to the ten wheeler running as the road engine. (Harrison Usher)

LOOKING LIKE a piece of Colorado narrow gauge, the mainline of the GN on the east side of Stevens Pass threads its way through the upper reaches of Tumwater Canyon in the 1900's. The line through Tumwater Canyon was abandoned by the railroad in 1929 after completion of the Chumstick line, and the railroad right of way is used today by U.S. Hwy, #2. (Harrison Usher)

TRAILING one of the little four wheel cabooses of the era and a bad order boxcar, the pusher engine of an east-bound drag rides the high steel across lower Martin Creek trestle in this 1905 scene. The long trestle, in continuous use from about 1900 (when it was rebuilt) until 1929, was not a place for anyone who feared heights. Its east end was located almost directly inside the entrance to Horseshoe tunnel, and crews coming out of the bore were faced with a ride over its dizzying heights just after leaving the dark dank confines of the almost circular tunnel. (Harrison Usher)

A ROTARY CHURNS ITS WAY through a small snowslide outside a snowshed "up on the hill" across from Scenic. A roadmaster, complete with derby hat, watches the operation from the small ledge alongside the mainline. (Harrison Usher)

TWO RIBBONS of steel run west out of snowshed #3, just a few miles from Wellington going downgrade toward the Martin Creek tunnel, through a long cut formed by the compacted snow. (Harrison Usher)

AN EASTBOUND FREIGHT working hard going upgrade, rumbles across upper Martin Creek trestle just after coming out of the famous Horseshoe Tunnel between upper and lower Martin Creek trestles. In this 1900 scene the engine on the point is probably one of the 4-8-0 types that were widely used in the Cascades. A pusher engine further back is still in the confines of the tunnel and the crew must have been getting a heavy dose of accumulated smoke and gas in the 1,500' long bore. (Harrison Usher)

ENGINE NO. 1918 posed with her train crew by the schoolhouse in Skykomish in 1913. Engineer Charley Andrews, holding the oil can, was the only man to actually see the avalanche in which over 100 people were killed at Wellington in 1910, come down off the mountain. Mr. Andrews deadheading back to Skykomish, had been sleeping in one of the coaches of the stalled trains, but because of a premonition of impending disaster had left the train and was standing between the station platform and trains when it hit. The avalanche, estimated to have been 1,000' wide and 15' high when it shot across the tracks, carrying everything in its path with it, rolling trains, structures, trees and catenary down into the valley. Mr. Andrews was among the first to help victims of the disaster and remained in engine service for many more years. (Claude Witt)

THE HIGH CASCADES were spectacular in their mantle of white as the fresh moist snow, particularly on the west side of the summit, clung to every surface—horizontal or vertical. The click of the wheels on the rail joints was reduced to a barely audible snick, muffled by the deep snow, but, train crews were not deceived by the quiet beauty of the landscape. More than one train popped into a snowshed barely in time to avoid a slide coming down, and proceeding from shed to shed was like moving from one safety island to the next. (Harrison Usher)

33

THE GREAT NORTHERN STEAMSHIP COMPANY organized by Hill in 1900, and the Great Northern Pacific Steamship Company organized in 1914 after the completion of the Spokane Portland & Seattle Railway (a joint venture of the GN & NP), were respectively: a Trans-Pacific carrier and an Oregon to California coastwise carrier. Here, the steamship Great Northern departs from Astoria, Oregon on its maiden voyage to San Francisco in 1915. Two sister ships joined the Great Northern in the same year.

The Minnesota and the Dakota were in service on the run to the Orient between Seattle, Yokohama and Hong Kong. All of the ships were sold by the end of the first World War, because the government began regulating the activities of the railroads through the Interstate Commerce Commission. (Great Northern Railway)

TRAVELERS could transfer from the GN's Wenatchee-Oroville branch line trains to the sternwheeler "Okanogan," shown here at Chelan Falls, Washington on the Columbia River in 1912, for points up river not served by the railroad. The sternwheelers were discontinued shortly after the branch line was completed to Oroville, Washington, on the Canadian border, in 1913. (Walt Thayer)

A FOUR WHEELED CABOOSE is shown at Spokane in 1914 on the Hillyard-Newport local. These four wheeled cabooses, were very similar to those used on the Burlington and the Lackawanna railroads, were widely used on the Great Northern until about the time of the first World War. These frail little bobbers, very light in weight and construction, were placarded "no pushers." They continued to be used for some years in work train service after their removal fom the mainline. (Claude Witt)

IN THIS TURN OF THE CENTURY PHOTO one of the old whaleback type ore boats, in vogue for some years on the Great Lakes, is shown ready to take on iron ore at the GN Allouez docks in Superior, Wisconsin. From this beginning in about 1906 the ore business of the Great Northern progressed to the point where in the 40's 16,000 ton ore trains coming down off the iron range were a standard operating procedure. (C. G. Nelson, GN Rwy.)

TEN WHEELER NO. 1061 heads up the International Limited, the morning train to Vancouver, B.C. The rectangular style of Great Northern herald, with slanted road name, first appeared on locomotive tenders about the time of the Alaska-Yukon-Pacific Exposition held in Seattle in 1909 and was used by the GN until about 1923 when it was replaced by the familiar Rocky Mountain Goat herald. (Great Northern Railway)

INTERIOR VIEW of the waiting room, King Street Station just after its opening in 1906. (Walt Grecula, GN Rwy.)

THE ELABORATE MOSAIC TILE COMPASS in the floor of the lobby of King Street Station, Seattle, was made of many thousands of pieces of tile individually cut and fitted into place with painstaking care. The street cars and carriages are long since gone but the station still remains in 1967. (Claude Witt)

GN TRAIN #1, later known as the Oriental Limited, slips easily down the west slope of the Cascade Mountains, below Stevens Pass, on a cool misty morning. Judging by the equipment, and the lack of a tailgate sign, the year is probably 1904 or early 1905.

In December 1905 the Great Northern put the Oriental Limited into service on a 58 hour schedule between St. Paul and Seattle. Although not a speed burner in the same sense that the 20th Century Limited or The Broadway Limited were in the east, between Chicago and New York, it was as fast as its contemporaries between Chicago and Los Angeles, and faster than the North Coast Limited on the neighboring Northern Pacific by nearly 4¼ hours. The Oriental Limited averaged 31 mph between St. Paul and Seattle, and considering the number of stops, and the mountains to be crossed this performance was quite remarkable for a railroad that was barely a decade old. (Great Northern Railway)

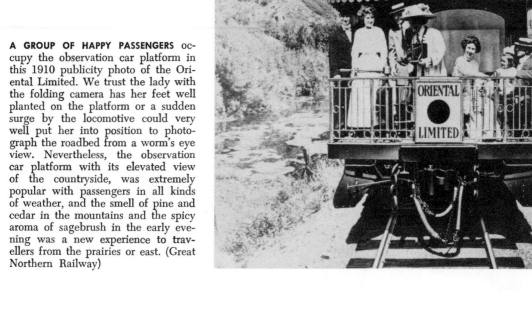

A GROUP OF HAPPY PASSENGERS occupy the observation car platform in
this 1910 publicity photo of the Oriental Limited. We trust the lady with
the folding camera has her feet well
planted on the platform or a sudden
surge by the locomotive could very
well put her into position to photograph the roadbed from a worm's eye
view. Nevertheless, the observation
car platform with its elevated view
of the countryside, was extremely
popular with passengers in all kinds
of weather, and the smell of pine and
cedar in the mountains and the spicy
aroma of sagebrush in the early evening was a new experience to travellers from the prairies or east. (Great
Northern Railway)

PICTURED HERE is the interior of the
observation car of the Oriental Limited in 1910, complete with stained
glass clerestory windows and electric
lighting. The photo has been heavily
re-touched but is accurate in detail
and illustrates the ornate interior of
passenger equipment prior to World
War I. (Great Northern Railway)

FROM EVERETT, WASHINGTON the GN follows the shore of Puget Sound for a distance of about 30 miles to gain a water level entrance into Seattle. The railroad winds around one sweeping curve after another with the gray green salt water on one side and the high fir studded bluffs on the other while sea gulls wheel and cry above the flats at low tide in search of clams and fish. Ocean going steamers, fishing boats, tugs with barges and ferry boats crisscross the sound while the trains hustle past. This is heavy duty mainline, both to the east, and to the province of British Columbia.

Here on a beautiful day in 1909, the year of the Alaska-Yukon-Pacific Exposition, the Oriental Limited, behind Baldwin built Pacific 1443, is on the last lap of its transcontinental journey to Seattle. The train had left Chicago three days and three nights before behind the power of the Burlington bound for St. Paul where the GN took over for the remaining 1,829 miles. Now on this fine morning the passengers give their luggage to the porters and latecomers in the dining car hurry to finish their breakfast for in a few minutes, with a clanging of the bell the train will pull into Seattle. (Great Northern Railway)

BARELY VISIBLE IN THE PHOTO, dated 1915, is the "See America First" slogan on the side of the open air car. This slogan, coined by Louis Hill, son of James J. Hill, has since become a part of the American lexicon. These open air sight-seeing cars, most of them rebuilds of outdated equipment, enjoyed a spell of popularity on the Northern Pacific, Canadian Pacific, Milwaukee Road and Great Northern operating during the daylight hours of the summer season in the Rockies. Their operation was widely advertised, by the railroads who had them, to attract tourist business, and in the days before vistadomes and great domes they were a definite attraction. Actually, cars very similar to these are in use today on the Rio Grande narrow gauge running to Silverton during the summer months. Passengers standing on the car steps, and others leaning out of the car, would give the safety engineer of today many qualms, but train speeds in 1915, particularly in the mountains, could hardly be called fast, and a member of the train crew was always present in the car to supervise the passengers. It would be difficult to find, even in this day, a finer way to view the magnificent scenery in the Rockies, and it is to be regretted that it is no longer possible to operate them behind the fast streamliners of today. (Great Northern Railway)

A BALDWIN BUILT MALLET, No. 1919, stands in the yards at Skykomish with an eastbound extra in 1913. At one time the Great Northern was the largest operator of Mallet types in the country and by 1908 22 of the 1800's and 1900's (all 2-6-6-2 types) were in service in the Cascades. These big fellows could slog all day at a steady 5 to 6 mph—provided the firemen could keep them hot. The Mallets were the answer, as far as the GN was concerned, to lifting heavy tonnage trains over the summit of the Cascades. These big compound engines were rated at 1600 tons on a 1 per cent grade, and something less than half of that on the 2.2% grades of the Cascade Division.

The long hickory club or "hickey" as it was called, in the hand of the brakeman standing on the pilot of No. 1919, was the trade badge of brakemen and was used as a lever between the spokes of the brake-wheel to help apply the hand brakes when the engineer (by whistle signal) called for them. Coming down the mountain with 1500 or so tons shoving behind the engine on the steep 2.2% grades was dangerous, with primitive air brakes, and when the engineer called for more brakes the brakemen would have to scramble from car to car setting them as quickly as possible before control was lost. During the day a fog of brakeshoe smoke would fill the air around a descending train, and at night rims of fire would often circle the wheels as the friction overheated wheels and brakeshoes. Stops were necessary every few miles to cool the wheels and prevent the brakeshoes from burning out. (Claude Witt)

DURING THE Alaska-Yugkon-Pacific Exposition in Seattle in 1909 the Great Northern had on display one of the "Big Mallet" engines used in the Cascades along with engine No. 1, the William Crooks. This postcard photo was published by the General Passenger Department in St. Paul and given away as a promotional piece for some years on the trains and in the ticket offices. (Walt Thayer)

No. 1909, the "BIG MALLET" and No. 1, the "WILLIAM CROOKS."
On exhibition at the Alaska-Yukon-Pacific Exposition, Seattle.
The largest engine used on the Great Northern Railway and its diminutive prototype. Average load capacity of the "Wm. Crooks" on a cent grade 60 tons; that of the "Big Mallet" 1600 tons. The "Big Mallet" hauls practically as much tonnage as twenty-five "Wm. Cro ¶ No. 1909, the "BIG MALLET." (Built in 1908) Weight on drivers 355,000 lbs. Total weight, engine and tender 530,20 Diameter of driving wheels 55 ins. 4 cylinders, 2 high pressure, 22½ ins. by 32 ins.; 2 low pressure, 33 ins. by 32 ins. ¶ No. 1 the " LIAM CROOKS." (Built in 1861) Weight on drivers 55,400 lbs. Diameter of driving wheels 63 ins. ¶ cylinder, 12 ins. by 2

TRAIN #27 the famed Fast Mail of the Great Northern, is shown at the division point of Troy, Montana with ten wheeler No. 1028 on the point in the summer of 1914, taking on water after coaling at the huge dock in the background. The engineer and a locomotive inspector are oiling around and examining the running gear, while car inspectors starting at the first mail storage car behind the engine, work their way back to the last car tapping wheels and running gear with their hammers, listening for an off key metallic thud which would indicate a metal fracture not visible to the naked eye. In the Railway Post Office car, in the middle of the train, the mail is sorted to be ready for morning delivery from post offices along the way. The only road, of the three northwest transcontinentals to hold a government contract for delivery of mail from St. Paul to Spokane and Seattle, the Great Northern's Fast Mail held the record, for many years, for the fastest long distance run in the world. Many of the GN passenger engines were designed with the demanding schedule of #27 in mind. (Claude Witt)

A BROOKS BUILT MOGUL (2-6-0 TYPE) backs the first passenger train into Omak, Washington on the Wenatchee-Oroville branch on June 2, 1913. The heavy wooden pilot built on the back of the Mogul's tender is evidence that Belpaire boilered No. 463 has seen service on the switchbacks in the Cascades. (Walt Thayer)

A NORTHBOUND PASSENGER TRAIN in the early 1920's crosses the Salmon Bay drawbridge over the ship canal between Seattle and the suburb of Ballard. The monstrous Bascule drawspan is still in service in the 1960's and provides the Great Northern with direct access to Seattle from the north along Puget Sound. (Great Northern Railway)

THE ROUNDHOUSE AT SKYKOMISH was a busy place when this photo was taken about 1912. Skykomish supplied both the road and helper engines for the long 21 mile grind up to Wellington and 2-8-0's, 4-8-0's, and 2-6-6-2's line the tracks into and out of the roundhouse. The hinged extensions on the stacks of the engines were used through the tunnels and snowsheds to help divert the smoke and gas but they didn't help much in the 2.6 mile long Cascade Tunnel before the electrics entered service in 1909. Smoke and heat were so bad that engines carried gas masks in later years but the crews long before this learned to soak cotton waste in water and breathe through it as a crude sort of gas mask. Heat in the cabs too was a problem and there are reports of cab temperature climbing to well over 150 degrees while in the bore. (Claude Witt)

TEN WHEELER NO. 1009 on the head end of train #27, The Fast Mail, in Spokane, Washington in 1914 poses with the train crew and the mail clerks who work in the RPO car on this part of the run.

Many a hair raising run was recorded by the Fast Mail for renewal of the government mail contract depended upon the on time performance of this train into Spokane and Seattle. At division points, fresh engines were ready and waiting for the arrival of #27, and the road engine was no sooner uncoupled and moving toward the roundhouse, than the fresh engine was backing down to couple to the waiting train with safety pops lifting from the full head of steam. Coupling was quickly completed, air tests made, and the train was high-balling out of the yard. On the occasions when The Fast Mail was running late the dispatcher put everything else into the hole, and cleared the entire railroad, if necessary, to get The Fast Mail through. While the engineer sought to regain lost time the clerks in the RPO car were in for a real ride as the cars swayed through the curves and rocketed down the tangents. Mountain running, in particular, required engineers who knew every curve, stretch of tangent, bridge and bluff on their division. Engineers had to know what track their engines would get through at maximum speed and what stretches of track, that due to curves or possible obstructions (like falling rock) needed more cautious running. A half century of continuing government mail contracts testify to the ability of these enginemen who pulled the throttle on The Fast Mail. (Claude Witt)

THIS WORLD WAR I PERIOD PHOTO of an eastbound passenger train pulling into Index, Washington has been the subject of much speculation. The style of the faint lettering on the photo would indicate that it is an early Pickett photo—Mr. Pickett lived in Index and had a small studio there. Very little can be determined concerning the event taking place, but the size of the crowd at the station is completely out of keeping with the size of the town. Possibly trouble on the line has forced these passengers to wait for the next train or maybe they are GN employees returning to Tye and other stations after a holiday. In any event, on this day, Index looks like a commuter station, and probably has not seen so many people at the station before or since. (Claude Witt)

IN 1921 THE GREAT NORTHERN experimented with an early form of "piggybacking" new cars on standard flat cars, and unloaded them at King Street Station using the new Whiting transfer crane. The experiment, moderately successful, still left much to be desired. The manpower needed to operate the crane and to prepare the car for unloading was costly, and a switch engine crew was tied up until the unloading was completed. Even though the idea was shelved for some years, it did represent a step forward in railroad technology, and the basic idea was revived and perfected in the 1950's, using the tri-level racks. (Great Northern Railway)

WITH THE SNOW CAPPED OLYMPIC MOUNTAINS in the background, a northbound passenger swings around the almost continual series of S curves along Puget Sound between Everett and Seattle in this photo taken in the 1920's by Lee Pickett of Index, Washington.

THE OLD 5,000 KILOWATT POWER PLANT located on the Wenatchee River, just west of Leavenworth, Washington, was built during the days of the original three phase electrification between Wellington and Cascade Tunnel Station. The water tank beside the powerhouse is actually a surge tank at the end of the 2 mile long, 8.5' diameter water supply pipe line to the generators. The pipe started at the low diverting built dam upriver. (C. G. Nelson, GN Rwy.)

ONE OF THE NEW P-2 CLASS Mountain type engines, just entering service on the Great Northern, is on public display on the team tracks next to King Street Station in Seattle in 1923. Brought out to Seattle for the occasion too was the William Crooks and its consist—the first passenger train to operate in Minnesota on the old First Division of the St. Paul & Pacific in June 1862. (Walt Grecula, GN Rwy.)

THE WILLIAM CROOKS poses for its picture in the yards at St. Paul in 1920 with the baggage car and coach that made up the first passenger train in Minnesota in 1862. The classic 4-4-0 (an American type) had driving wheels of 63″ diameter and an overall length of 51′. Complete with tender it weighed 40 tons. In comparison, an O-8 Mikado built in 1932, put a weight of almost 41 tons on one driving axle, and the Vanderbilt tender of an R-2, 2-8-8-2 was nearly as long as the entire William Crooks complete with tender. Carefully preserved by the Great Northern, the William Crooks, today is on permanent display in St. Paul Union Depot. (Great Northern Railway)

WITH A BRACE OF THE EARLY B-B ELECTRICS on the head end, the Oriental Limited of 1921 gets underway out of Tye, headed for the old Cascade Tunnel and then the small yard at Cascade Tunnel Station. The electrics will be cut out at Cascade Tunnel Station after a run of something less than 5 miles. Forest fires have denuded the mountainside rising above Tye presenting a grim desolate scene, not typical of the beautiful and rugged North Cascades. (C. G. Nelson, GN Rwy.)

A GREAT NORTHERN CONSTRUCTION TRAIN, used in installing the new catenary from Skykomish to Cascade Tunnel Station in the late 1920's is shown along the mainline near the summit of Stevens Pass. The unusual four wheel cabooses were used in mainline service on the Cascade Division for many years. Note that these cabooses—used only in construction and work train service after about 1918—were not built with end ladders for access to the roof. Small doors were built in the ends of the cupola for access to the roof and emergency doors were located in the sides of the cupola in place of the usual sliding side windows. (C. G. Nelson, GN Rwy.)

THE YEARS OF MODERN STEAM POWER

Certainly one of the major reasons for the interest evident in steam locomotives of the Great Northern is their distinctive—almost unique—appearance. The steam power of many railroads, except for the road names, were as alike as peas in a pod and painted one color—black. The different appearance of GN steam power was due in large part to the Belpaire firebox (introduced to the road in 1898 on Brooks Works 4-8-0's) that imparted a squarish look to the last part of the boiler. While it didn't enhance the appearance of the locomotive, it did make it distinctive. The GN along with the Pennsylvania Railroad, was the only major user of the Belpaire design in this country. There were two exceptions in later years, the Baldwin built P-2 class 4-8-2 and S-2 class 4-8-4 delivered in 1923 and 1929 respectively. They used the conventional radial stay firebox and with their smoothly rounded boilers they were probably the best looking passenger engines on the GN. Freight power, whether ordered from outside builders or built in GN shops, was with only one exception, fitted with Balpaire fireboxes.

In the 1920's the Great Northern began adding another feature that was to become a hallmark of large GN power, the Vanderbilt tender. The first engines to be equipped with this big cylindrical tank were the P-2 class Mountain and Q-1 class 2-10-2. In short order the R-1, R-2, S-1, S-2 and O-8 classes followed, all equipped with large capacity Vanderbilt tenders. While some of these engines burned oil and others burned coal, the tenders outwardly were nearly identical in appearance.

Coincident with delivery of the new engines the GN also started applying the famous "Billy Goat" herald to the large tapered side sheets of the tenders fuel compartment. The GREAT NORTHERN name was removed from the sides of the water compartment and the red and while herald painted on the black background of the tender added a touch of color to what had been just another black tender trailing a locomotive. The herald had been used for some years on freight equipment but the application to locomotive tenders did much to publicize the Great Northern as well as to brighten up the motive power.

In 1925 the new R-1 class 2-8-8-2 locomotives were being delivered to the Great Northern by Baldwin Locomotive Works. These monsters were not only the first 2-8-8-2's ordered by the road, they were the first modern locomotives on the GN to have two compound air pumps mounted on the front of the smokebox. This feature not only gave better weight distribution and balance to the engine (with the heavy pumps mounted opposite each other) it created another part of the "GN look" that would become so familiar on the R-2, S-1, S-2, O-8 and rebuilt N-3 class 2-8-8-0's. Now only two logical places remained on these engines to mount the headlight, centered under the pumps on the rigid frame types, or out on the pilot deck of the articulateds. This low slung headlight combined with the large pumps gave a powerful appearance to the front of the locomotives, so that rather light engines like the S-2, appeared bigger and heavier than they really were. In the case of the O-8 class 2-8-2's, which were big boilered and massive to begin with, the pump heavy smokebox added a fierce look of brute power and tremendous reserve strength.

In common with other railroads that had older, but still serviceable, engines on the active roster, not all of the Great Northern engines were handsome or powerful in appearance. Some, like the class H-4 Pacifics, built by Lima in 1914 did not age gracefully. With their high perched rectangular cabs and small teardrop shaped headlight that hung far out over the pilot, long boilered and lean with low mounted running boards, shotgun stacked, fitted with delicate looking 73″ drivers that had odd wedge shaped counterbalances between the spokes of the main drivers, they were far from the classic design of some Pacifics. Through many shoppings and modifications over the years the H-4's evolved into a fragile looking locomotive. They might have at least partially escaped such an appearance if the tender had been better proportioned and more smoothly countered. However, trailing the H-4 was one of the little rectangular, outside braced tenders peculiar to the GN and the Burlington. Function decreed that the outside braces on the fuel compartment be arched across the top of the tender, but this created the overall impression of a rolling rose arbor.

IN 1940 steam is still the prime mover of freight and passenger trains and in this scene as old as railroading itself, the fireman on a switcher fills the water compartment after the engineer has spotted the engine under the water plug. (Casey Adams)

GN Pacifics, by and large, were good serviceable locomotives, Some, in later years were fitted with trailing truck boosters and performed yeoman service, on freight assignments, while others, in light passenger service during the 1930's and 40's powered many of the name trains of the Great Northern.

None of the Pacifics had the classic design of the USRA designed Pacifics of the Southern Railway or the simple efficient business-like design of the Pennsylvania's Belpaire boilered K-4's, but many had a beauty all their own with the aluminum painted smokebox, light olive green boiler, and the gloss black tender that carried that magnificent big red and white herald. What the older power lacked in symmetrical design and balance it made up for in the beautifully maintained color scheme that was the pride of the road for years. The GN has long been noted as a "good housekeeper" and the engines, whether new or old, reflected this policy.

Baldwin Locomotive Works, without question, was the favorite builder of the Great Northern and the road turned to Baldwin time after time both for new types of locomotives, and the re-orders, as successive improvements were made. From as far back as 1900 Lima and Alco between them, managed to get a crack at building barely three dozen locomotives. Lima built a few of the class H-4 Pacifics and Alco built a dozen or so Mikados in the O-2 and O-3 classes. The GN shops accounted for a number of new locomotives including the O-8's and R-2's.

GN power was, by and large, conservative in design and the road seemed reluctant to accept wheel arrangements that detracted from the weight that could be put on the drivers. The GN's far north neighbor, the Northern Pacific, tried, accepted, and then operated a large fleet of Challengers that were among the most modern locomotives in the world. In 1939 the GN purchased two Challengers, #4000 and 4001. However, these engines quickly found their way onto the Spokane, Portland, & Seattle Railway (GN-NP owned subsidiary) through a lease arrangement and so far as can be determined never did operate on the east-west GN mainline. These two locomotives were the only freight engines the GN ever owned that possessed either a four wheel lead or trailing truck. Instead of this approach to articulated freight power, the GN concentrated on 2-8-8-0's, 2-8-8-2's, and 2-6-8-0's. These locomotives respectively were: the most modern 2-8-8-0's in the country, the most powerful 2-8-8-2's, and 2-6-8-0's had the most unusual wheel arrangement.

In the estimation of many, the peak of steam development was reached in 1931/32, when the O-8 Mikados were built in the GN shops. They were super power GN style, developing 75,900 lbs. of tractive effort (without the complications of a booster) while rolling on the biggest drivers (69″) ever put on a GN freight engine. They could pull like a dray horse and thanks to the big boilers (from scrapped 2-6-8-0's) had ample reserve capacity to work full out at speeds of 50 mph. No Mike in the country could match their overall performance. They were a tribute to the skill and ingenuity of the motive power design department of the GN and to the craftsmanship of the Hillyard shops. They were also the last of the GN steam designs, although for some years the shops would continue in a rebuild and modernization capacity.

THE FIREMAN ON #2516 has the waterspout buried in waterhatch of the Vanderbilt tender and will not shut off the water until it overflows down the curved sides. In the days of steam operation the water stop at Scenic was important, for here, the railroad crossed the Tye river and curved to the other side of the valley to begin the long climb back to the west before crossing Martins Creek and reversing direction through the Horseshoe tunnel to continue east again. The 2.2% grade never eased until the train stopped at Tye for the change to electric power. On this long hard climb steam engines consumed copious quantities of water and filling the tank at Scenic was mandatory. (Lee Pickett)

A CLASS A-9 YARD GOAT steams softly in the dead of night at Minot waiting for the crew to begin the third shift. When diesels began to replace steam power in 1939 the little elderly Class A switchers, remembered with a genuine affection in yards from Superior to Bellingham, were among the first to permanently drop their fires. With safety valves popping they registered a steam pressure of only 160 lbs. Most burned coal and were hand bombers, not difficult to fire, but dirty to work on. Some of the Class A's dated back to the 1880's and with barely 25,000 lbs. of tractive effort they were simply outdated. (Casey Adams)

JUST A STEP AWAY FROM THE BONEYARD in 1941, a little Mogul dating back to 1896, no longer fit for mainline or branchline duties has been downgraded to light switching duties. Used as a yard switcher, the diminutive Class D engine wheezes around the yard at Minot until the need for new flues or other heavy repairs sends it to be scrapped. Judging by the condition of the paint on the tender, the proud GN herald has been absent for some time, a further clue to its now lowly status and ultimate destiny. (Casey Adams)

THE OLDEST ENGINES STILL IN SERVICE on the GN in 1940 were a few of the American types built in 1883. A pair of them, No. 199 and 103 are shown outside the roundhouse at Hillyard, Washington between assignments on the Kettle Falls branch. Engine No. 199 was transferred to the Minot Division, and when the diesels entered service was re-numbered No. 219. As No. 219 the little engine was the oldest engine on the Minot Division. (W. R. McGee and Casey Adams)

A HALF CENTURY OLD when this photo was taken in 1941, Class F-1 Consolidation, an 1892 graduate of the Brooks Works, provides the power for the Neihart local out of Great Falls, Montana. This ancient little kettle, that once ran in the Cascades, had been progressively downgraded through the years until it is now used for the lightest of way freight work. (W. R. McGee)

TEN WHEELER NO. 927 LEADS TRAIN #31 into St. Cloud, Minnesota on a crisp fall day in October, 1941. The little train ran between Sandstone and Willmar, Minnesota a distance of 135 miles on a 5¾ hr schedule, a snail's pace by 1967 standards, but not too bad considering that there were 26 stops involved in this distance. The old wooden mail car and coach were typical of branch line equipment from Minnesota to Washington. (W. R. McGee)

NO. 1053 at Minot, N.D. in the summer of 1941 was one of the last active ten wheelers on the Great Northern. Six months later, in March of 1942, all of the type had been scrapped or were in dead storage awaiting final disposition. The little 4-6-0 with tall rather delicate appearing 73″ drivers has coupled behind its tank an auxiliary water car that will allow it to pass at least a few water plugs. (Casey Adams)

BY 1942 ONLY ONE ENGINE of the ten Class K Atlantics, built by Baldwin in 1906 remained on the GN roster— No. 1707 on the Wilmar (Minnesota) Division. Originally built without a trailing truck (the trailing wheels were frame mounted, like C&NW 4-4-2's) they acquired Delta trailing trucks during modernizing programs. Balancing of the running gear was always troublesome and many unusual combinations of counterweights were applied. One of the really rare types, built first as balanced compounds and later simpled, they were fast but very light passenger power, and before 1925 powered the Oriental Limited across the more level districts. (Casey Adams)

55″ DRIVERED TWELVE WHEELERS (4-8-0's) were widely used on the GN just after completion of the mainline in 1893. 105 of them were ordered from Brooks and Rogers Locomotive Works between 1891 and 1900. Divided into five sub-classes, the Class G locomotives were heavy freight and pusher power for a number of years in the Cascades. As heavier and more powerful types entered service in the Pacific Northwest, the twelve wheelers began to appear in increasing numbers on the Dakota and Willmar Divisions. The Butte Division also operated a number of the class during World War II, and 8 of the original 105, were still in standby service as late as 1950. (Casey Adams)

AT MINOT, N.D. TWELVE WHEELER NO. 726, complete with archbar trucks on the tender and old square steam chests above the cylinders, prepares to receive a load of coal. The condition of the locomotive belies its true age. Built around the turn of the century, it has received excellent care, and rebuilding and modernizing programs through the years have altered the original lines and further disguised its age. Solid and substantial freight power, the 4-8-0's were popular with the GN for many years. (Casey Adams)

BEAUTIFUL LITTLE CLASS F CONSOLIDATION at Minot in 1940 shows the care lavished on the engine during an overhaul in the backshops. The bright aluminum painted smokebox was typical of engines assigned to the Minot Division. Note that the cylinder saddle and covers are painted black, on other Divisions the saddle was often painted olive green, while the cylinder covers on many passenger engines were either chromed or painted aluminum. (Casey Adams)

CLASS F-8 CONSOLIDATION NO. 1147, built by Rogers in 1903, has received class I repairs at Hillyard in 1950 and is being prepared for duty again. The electrician on the tender is reconnecting the electric conduit that carries power for the back-up light mounted on the tank.

This particular class of engine was used as standard freight power in the Cascades for years with the big Class L Mallets assisting as pushers and helpers. Capable of a fair turn of speed, the Consolidations also helped in passenger service. Good uncomplicated serviceable power, developing a tractive effort of around 49,000 lbs. and mounted on 55″ drivers, the Consolidations were purchased in large numbers by the GN shortly after the turn of the century, and as late as 1950, 36 of the Class F-8's were still on the active roster. (Wally Swanson)

IN 1953 THE GREAT NORTHERN gave to the city of Seattle the last active steam engine on the Cascade Division, Consolidation No. 1246 a Class F-8 Baldwin built in 1907 which had outlasted all of its bigger brothers on the Cascade Division and very nearly outlasted even the electrics. This was done at the suggestion of Post Intelligencer columnist Doug Welch. The engine was shopped at Interbay, carefully restored to better than new appearance and then moved to Woodland Park where it was put on ballasted 115 lb. rail within a protective enclosure. Here it may be seen today thanks to Doug Welch and the Park Board Commissioners. (Great Northern Railway)

O-1 CLASS MIKE, the first on the GN, waits on the ready track at Interbay roundhouse in Seattle. Often used as a pusher behind the monstrous 2-8-8-2's on the long 1% grade from Goldbar to Skykomish the 2-8-2 sports extra heavy tires that have increased the diameter of its drivers to 63″, standard on all Mikes except the O-8's. Lack of engine number boards beside the stack indicates that this photo was taken prior to 1941/42 when except for steam switchers, the number boards were applied to all GN power. (Walt Mendenhall)

A SOUTHBOUND FREIGHT behind a hardworking Mike passes the Canadian town of Whiterock, B.C. just across the international boundary at Blaine, Washington. GN rails here, through acquisition, and trackage rights over the Canadian National, reach directly into Vancouver, B.C. some 30 miles north of the border. (Robert G. Johnson)

WITH 55" DRIVERS PEDDLING FURIOUSLY, GN 1981 West races NP 5104 West near Helena, Montana. Although the low wheeled GN 2-6-8-0 is only pulling 8 cars and the "Billy Goat" is dead game the contest won't last long because NP 5104 from which this photograph was taken is a huge dual purpose 4-6-6-4 Challenger, rolling on roller bearing equipped 69" drivers. (W. R. McGee)

A WAY FREIGHT switching in the yards at Everett has just picked up loads of logs destined for the lumber mills in Seattle. The heavy log cars are straining the old engine and it exhausts enormous clouds of smoke into the clear morning air with every driver revolution. (Stuart B. Hertz)

FROM THE RAILFANS' VIEWPOINT the class M-2 2-6-8-0 articulateds were the most unusual engines in service on the GN. They were first built in 1910 as Mallet compounds to serve as pushers and helpers in the Cascades. Rebuilt in 1927 as simple engines their weight and boiler pressure were increased until they exerted over 102,000 lbs. of tractive effort. The GN was thrifty in its use of old engines and many of the M2's provided boilers for the 0-7 and 0-8 class Mikes in the thirties. With the huge facility at Hillyard, Washington available, engines were built and rebuilt until little of the original engine remained.

The M-2 was not a handsome engine and the unusual 2-6-8-0 wheel arrangement had little to do with its overall appearance. Some fitted with Vanderbilt tanks and lowered headlights were better looking than others, but No. 1967 with its old fashioned bandstand type of pilot deck, straight top boiler, Belpaire firebox, assorted outside plumbing, side mounted pumps, and high mounted headlight, trailed by the outside braced rectangular tender was an aparition.

Some enginemen called them "grasscutters" because of the flailing action of the large slab side rods around the 55″ drivers. Essentially the M-2's were slow speed locomotives and any atempt to push the speed was hard on the engine and track. Rough riding at any speed above 25 mph they vibrated with a fierce clatter of gangway plates and jingle of cab gauges. As one engineer put it, "I couldn't even keep my shoelaces tied."

In later years M-2's saw heavy service as road engines between Great Falls and Butte, Montana. On other parts of the system they were used in mine and oil train service or anywhere that required heavy pulling power and little speed. Although 11 of the class were still in limited service in 1950, they were largely phased out of service after World War II and except for the war would probably have finished their careers much sooner. (Casey Adams)

ELDERLY (LIMA 1914) coal burning, 73″ drivered Class H-4 Pacific, shows the ravages of time and many shoppings over the years. The odd counterbalance weights on the main drivers indicate attempts by the shops to lessen the rail pounding (dynamic augment) that could be quite severe at medium to high speed, a fault noted in several of the older classes of steam power, such as the Atlantics and 2-10-2's. Odd shaped sand and steam domes were a hallmark of older GN power, as was the outside braced tender. In subsequent rebuildings the features that did not affect the efficiency of the locomotive were often left "as is" and the appearance of the locomotive suffered accordingly. (Casey Adams)

M-2 CLASS 2-6-8-0 No. 1981 at the coaling dock in Minot, N.D. has the extra markers in place behind the classification lamps, and after the hostler finishes checking a loose fitting, it will move to the outbound lead to pick up its train. During World War II some of these elderly, but still serviceable, old hogs were moved from their usual haunt on the Butte Division to various power short divisions, straying as far east as the Minot Division and as far west as the Spokane Division.

No. 1981 had its appearance improved a great deal by moving the headlight to the pilot deck and acquiring a modern Vanderbilt tank. The new tank nearly overwhelmed the engine, small for an articulated, actually no longer than a Class Q 2-10-2. The unusual wheel arrangement had very little to do with the overall appearance of the engine, and the 55″ wheels were nearly hidden by the huge boiler and assorted running gear. Their rough riding characteristics could be traced to the last set of massive counterweighted drivers almost directly under the cab. Devoid of a trailing truck that would have eased the ride somewhat, the old hogs while backing up met every rail joint and switch point head on, and changed the angle of direction with a very positive lurch. Still, with all their faults, they could move tonnage—not very fast to be sure—but between Butte and Great Falls they would come slogging up the grade under a vast canopy of smoke and cinders while the front bandstand articulated to the curves and the exhaust bounced off the hills and mountainsides. (Casey Adams)

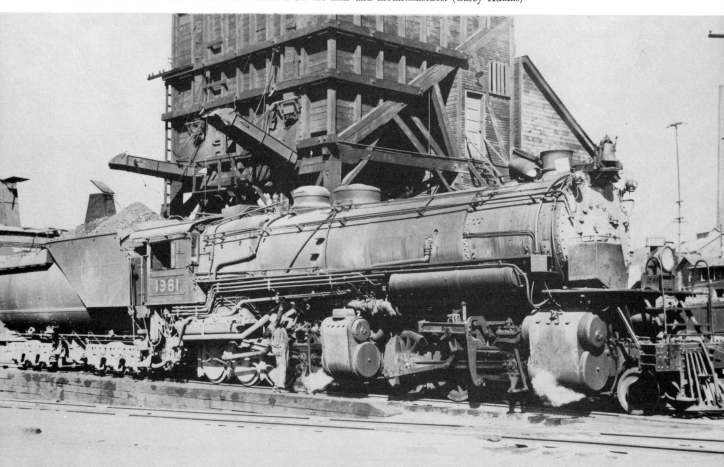

ONE OF THE 15 ENGINES in the Q-2 class, 2-10-2 No. 2185, originally built by Lima in 1914 and modernized by the railroad after delivery of the Q-1's in 1923, has been upgraded to modern specifications. It has lost many of its original identifying features such as the square cab, side mounted pumps and small rectangular tank, but a clue to its true age may be found in the old hat shaped boiler dome, and the humpback appearance of the boiler itself. A real "freight hog" in every sense of the word, slow, powerful (76,250 lbs. tractive effort), rough riding, devoid of roller bearings or modern cross counter balancing. Possessed with a voracious appetite for coal and water, the Q-2 was typical of pre-World War II drag freight power on many railroads. Built like the rock of Gibraltar, simple to repair with unsophisticated equipment, although requiring continual maintenance, they were greatly loved by many of the engine crews. Q-2's were used systemwide, although confined to their respective divisions, they rode the turntables in Minot and St. Paul as well as in Seattle and Spokane. (Great Northern Railway)

COAL BURNING 2-10-2 No. 2108, one of the Q-1 class has been called for an assignment and at almost the last moment it has been discovered that the sander valves are stuck. Help has arrived and the two mechanics, after a brief consultation about the vagaries of sander valves, and 2108's in particular, the valves are being freed. No. 2108 will jolt the extra eastbound freight into motion as called. (Casey Adams)

ON A MAGNIFICENT SUMMER MORNING in the early 1940's the southbound "Owl", overnight train from Vancouver, B.C. sprints along the shore of Puget Sound en route to Seattle. Due to arrive at 7 A.M. the train is running late because of heavy traffic on the north end, and Pacific No. 1363 is "picking them up and laying them down" in a race against time. (Stuart B. Hertz)

READY FOR ASSIGNMENT during the wheat rush or temporarily stored awaiting heavy repairs in the GN shops at Minot, locomotives line the tracks alongside the main in the summer of 1941. Most of the engines are Class Q 2-10-2's but a variety of power stretches ahead of Vanderbilt and rectangular tanks as far as the viaduct crossing over the railroad. In the middle foreground engine No. 3076 a Class O-1 Mike trailing a tank resembling a steel blockhouse nudges up to a newer Vanderbilt tank that is considerably higher and larger than the boiler on the 1911 model 2-8-2. (Casey Adams)

IT IS NOT DIFFICULT to see in this 1930 photograph of the eastbound Oriental Limited close by the Kootenai River, why the passenger train, particularly in the thinly populated Far West, was the most popular form of travel when any distance had to be covered. U.S. highways in the Northwest, except in the more densely populated areas, were still rugged—dusty and rough in dry weather, muddy and nearly impassable in wet weather. Automobiles, generally, were not capable of the sustained speeds that they are today, even if the highways had permitted such speed, and long distance buses were just coming into general use. Train speeds in this rugged country had to allow for the grades, curves, frequent scheduled stops and changes of power and crew at division points, but by comparison with other forms of transportation the trains were still the fastest as well as the most comfortable and reliable form of transportation available. (Lee Pickett)

GN #5 the westbound Cascadian hurries along the fast track between Wenatchee and Spokane just beyond the small town of Ephrata in May 1941. Much of Central Washington in the days before completion of the Columbia Basin Reclamation project was a thinly populated semi-dessert of brown hills, sagebrush, hot winds, jackrabbits and rattlesnakes. The land has since bloomed with a variety of green crops and the towns have boomed, so that this photo indicative of its character 25 years ago no longer holds true. (W. R. McGee)

CLASS H-6 PACIFIC No. 1714, running with a clear stack, peddles along the double mainline bordering Puget Sound with a solid consist of empty oil tankers en route to the big oil facility at Richmond Beach, just north of Seattle. The Pacific is well suited to this freight assignment with its 69″ drivers and well balanced running gear. Versatile, modernized, free steaming and easy riding, they were popular with the crews, and on the nearly level track from Seattle north to Vancouver, B.C., handled nearly every type of train from the Internationals to freights and work train extras. (Walt Mendenhall)

AT EVERETT, WASHINGTON the hogger of the northbound International Limited looks back along the length of the train for the conductor's highball. The lower platform is for the use of the north and southbound trains while the upper platform, alongside the station, serves the east west mainline. Just beyond the north end of the station the upper line turns and heads due east after passing through a tunnel under the business section of Everett. (Stuart B. Hertz)

SLOWLY SWINGING ON THE TURNTABLE at Minot, N.D. roundhouse in 1941, 2-10-2 No. 2109 freshly serviced and with a bunker full of coal, will be spotted on the ready track awaiting the next assignment. The big boilered Q-1, built by Baldwin in 1923 was fitted with 63" drivers and had a tractive effort of 76,251 pounds. Q-1 and Q-2 class 2-10-2's were best suited to drag service, and rarely ran faster than about 40 mph due to heavy dynamic augment and locomotive vibration. The shops at Great Falls and Hillyard made remarkable improvements in the locomotives' performance in 1946 when better methods of counterbalancing were developed but with diesels being delivered in increasing numbers technological improvements in steam power was akin to beating a dead horse. (Casey Adams)

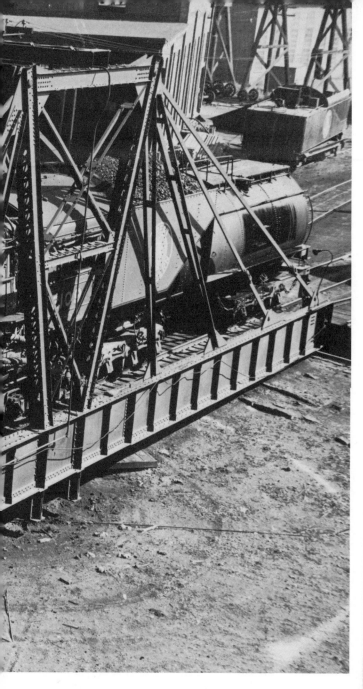

ALONG THE BANKS of the Kootenai River near Troy, Montana The Fast Mail, train No. 28, hurries eastward with 8 cars of mail and express. The Pacific on the head end is making light work of the consist on this almost level subdivision, but at Whitefish, with the long ascent through Marias Pass ahead, heavier power will replace the Pacific. (W. R. McGee)

THE NORTHBOUND INTERNATIONAL LIMITED, en route to Vancouver, B.C. leaves a light haze of oil smoke behind, as it rolls along the shores of Puget Sound south of Bellingham, Washington. (Stuart B. Hertz)

TRAIN NUMBER 27 the westbound Fast Mail, with a Pacific on the point, sweeps around a long curve near Kootenai Falls, Montana. Running on a limited schedule between St. Paul and Havre, Montana, number 27 became a local with 20 regular and 73 conditional (flag) stops scheduled in the intervening 530 miles between Havre and Spokane, Washington. In 1941, when this photo was taken by W. R. McGee, number 27 operated on a schedule that was carded three hours faster than the Empire Builder between St. Paul and Seattle. At one time number 27 was the fastest long distance run in the world, and the demanding schedule was one of the reasons for the purchase of the 4-8-4 type by the road in 1929/30.

WITH THE HOGGER PEERING DOWN at the deck structure of a new steel bridge being constructed over the Stillaguamish River near Silvana, Washington the International Limited, obeying a slow order, sets the new steel deck to drumming on the temporary wooden piling. The light Pacific and the following cars will see only a few more years service (until 1950) before being replaced by the new streamlined diesel powered equipment on order. (Stuart B. Hertz)

A CLASS H-5 PACIFIC built by the GN shops in 1926/27 from Class E-14 ten wheelers hurries northbound along Puget Sound with the morning train to Vancouver, B.C. Head-end business is heavy on this fine summer day and three Railway Express Agency (baggage) cars and an R.P.O. car are cut in between the engine and the following coaches. The 73″ drivered H-5's were the most numerous of the Pacific type sub classes and they powered at various times, every passenger run on the Great Northern. As late as 1950 twenty four of the class were still in service, although relegated to light freight, mixed, and occasional passenger service. (Stuart B. Hertz)

EXTRA 1369 EAST rolls through Chinook, Montana with 14 cars in May of 1946. The Pacific on the point, now trailing a Vanderbilt tank is better looking than most of the class that still used the older rectangular tenders, and the solid type lead truck wheels are more modern appearing than the older spoked style. The only real clues to the age of the engine (Baldwin 1910) are the old high domes and semi-shotgun stack and a cab that is huge, compared to the diameter of the boiler. (W. R. McGee)

A WHITE FACED MOUNTAIN gets the westbound Builder underway out of Whitefish, Montana in April 1940. During the late thirties and early forties the power assigned to passenger runs on the Kalispell Division had their smokeboxes painted a silvery white and some of the locomotives were further decorated with oxide or mineral red cab roofs and window frames. This combined with the light olive green boilers and cylinder saddles has since become known as "The Glacier Park Color Scheme." (W. R. McGee)

BALDWIN BUILT CLASS C-1 0-8-0 heavy switcher was the most powerful of the five sub-classes of 0-8-0's purchased by the GN during and just after World War I. Possessing a tractive effort of 61,430 lbs. the 0-8-0's continued in service long after the 0-6-0's, and with the even more powerful diesels ruled the large yards and handled transfer cuts. Some of the class (like No. 813) were coal burners while others were equipped to burn oil. (Casey Adams)

THE FIREMAN AND ENGINEER of a 2-8-8-0 are faced with a dilemma of minor proportions as the waterspout just used in filling the tank has wedged itself between the handrails while being swung out of the way. Much pushing and shoving has been to no avail and the situation will be resolved only after more effort and some calling on greater powers will be invoked. (Casey Adams)

RECENTLY OVERHAULED oil burning Class C-1 switcher No. 839 steams softly in the yards at Minot before moving out into the yard on classification duties. (Casey Adams)

ONE OF THE BEST LOOKING ENGINES on the GN was the Baldwin built Class P-2 Mountain type. The 28 engines of this class were built in 1923 for service on the Oriental Limited, the Fast Mail and Silk trains. Very conventional in appearance the P-2's along with the S-2's were the only locomotives on the road with conical boilers. Although not as fast as the Northerns, they were capable of speeds around 70 mph. They were fitted with 73″ drivers, and in tractive effort were only slightly less powerful than an S-2 (57,580 lbs. to 58,305 lbs.) but couldn't, of course, sustain this power as well in the higher speed ranges because of their smaller boilers and fireboxes. In a modernization program after the war, half of the class were equipped with roller bearings increasing their ability to sustain higher speeds without running hot in the driving boxes or pins, a trouble common on most any conventional bearing engine. The GN was the only Northwest transcontinental to use a Mountain type. Even after delivery of the Northerns the P-2 Mountains continued to be used on the Builder and Fast Mail, supplementing the bigger engines rather than being replaced by them in first class service. (Casey Adams)

FROM THE GREAT NORTHERN "GOAT" of February 1927 is reprinted this photo of heavyweight champion, Gene Tunney, posing on the observation platform of the Oriental Limited. Note the tailgate sign mounted on the back railing of the platform. During this era of the twenties the Great Northern goat—facing forward was called "Old Bill." Today, the goat is known as "Rocky, the Great Northern goat" and appears in a side silhouette, without any facial detail. (Great Northern Railway)

THE ORIENTAL LIMITED in 1930 heads east through the Pend Oreille River Valley in Idaho behind a P-2 Mountain type. The express reefers behind the engine carrying fresh salmon from the coast to eastern markets were equipped with special racks for this purpose. GN & CB&Q express reefers were cut into the head end of the Oriental or Builder on every eastbound trip when the salmon were in season. The delicate flavor and firm flesh of the famous King salmon commanded premium prices in the east and these carload shipments moved on the fastest schedules. (Lee Pickett)

THE "SANDPOINT TURN" local freight returning to Newport, Washington behind a backing 2-8-2, No. 3136 and eastbound extra behind 4-8-2 No. 2524 coming up the valley are about to pass here at Laclede, Idaho in the beautiful Pend Oreille River Valley. (Dr. Philip R. Hastings)

AGAINST A BACKDROP OF MOUNTAINS, the westbound Cascadian is led by big boilered Mountain No. 2506 out of the west end of the yards at Goldbar in this foreshortened and dramatic photo of steam in the Cascades. (Everett Herald Photo)

82

WITH BLACK OIL SMOKE shooting up from the stubby stack freight extra 2524 East blasts into deep rock cuts along the Pend Oreille River in Idaho. The conical boilered 4-8-2 has acquired a larger tank for extended runs without refueling, and has recently been released from passenger assignments in this 1950 scene. Falling rock is a hazard in this area, and slide detector fences connected to the block signals line the right of way. (Dr. Philip R. Hastings)

ON MARCH 11, 1928, along the Wenatchee River near Peshastin, Washington a P-2 class Mountain on the head end of the westbound Oriental Limited hit a rock resulting in the engine's derailment. Fortunately, because the train was running slowly the only damage other than to the engine was the lifting off of the baggage/mailcar from its front truck bolster. It was some time however, before the big Mountain was put back on the rails and pulled back to Wenatchee for repairs. (Lee Pickett)

JAMMED AGAINST THE CYLINDERS of the 4-8-2 on the head end of the Oriental Limited is part of the large rock that caused its derailment. The pilot and running board ladders were smashed by the impact but damage is relatively light and the major task in this accident will be in picking the engine out of the river without further damage. (Lee Pickett)

MOUNTAIN TYPE No. 2527 in the shops at Minot, North Dakota for heavy repairs and overhaul has most of its bridgelike frame exposed while the drivers and rods are being worked on in another part of the backshops. Minot's large, fully equipped shops and roundhouse, capable of most any repair or overhaul function, were second only to the Jackson Street shops in St. Paul on the east end of the system. (Casey Adams)

THE EMPIRE BUILDER, train No. 2 eastbound, crosses the Spokane River in early morning, having left Seattle at 10 P.M. the night before, behind a Mountain type steam engine. The 13 car train changed to electrics at Sky-komish and back again to steam at Wenatchee. Now behind Mountain No. 2502 it will probably change power again at Spokane, before continuing east. (W. R. McGee)

HARD ON THE MARKERS of an inbound passenger train ahead, a freight bound for Interbay yard, north of King Street station, drifts slowly along the mainline, while waiting for the passenger to clear the throat switches leading to the station platforms. Once the passenger is clear, the 4-8-2 will pull by the station on the freight track and if the interlocking signals are clear will pass through the tunnel under Seattle and on the short distance to Interbay. (Stan Gray)

WITH THE RAYS OF THE SETTING SUN reflecting off the number boards and headlight Mountain No. 2524 passes a semaphore indicating stop for westbound traffic. The eastbound local freight to Sandpoint, Idaho is running parallel to the Pend Oreille River in this at dusk scene by famed railroad photographer, Dr. Philip R. Hastings.

THE MAILMAN of the Great Northern, The Fast Mail #27, slams through Columbia Falls, Montana behind a white faced P-2 class Mountain. The handsome 4-8-2's were conventional in layout and design, and were not changed much from the day they were built in 1923. They were good engines in the opinion of GN enginemen in either freight or passenger service. Free steaming, easy riding and without bad habits they came about as close to a USRA type as any engine on the "Big G." (W. R. McGee)

TRAIN #408 leaving Union Station at Tacoma, Washington is heading for Portland, Oregon over the joint NP-UP-GN mainline that follows Puget Sound nearly to Olympia, Washington. Just visible through the smoke is an NP engine on the approach to the old "Prairie Line" out through South Tacoma. (Stuart B. Hertz)

NO. 2033, a 1925 vintage R-1 is shown in Minot August 22, 1941 with train 449 hauling 125 westbound empty reefers. One of the four Baldwin built R-1 class locomotives, it was identical to the 1928 GN built R-1's and not too noticeably different in appearance from the 1929/30 GN built R-2's. The R-2 locomotives were fitted with a Delta trailing truck, larger tender and a vestibule cab. They were somewhat heavier than the R-1's (1,059,220 lbs. compared to 945,720 lbs.) and were quite a bit more powerful with a tractive effort of 142,055 lbs. to the R-1's 129,622 lbs. due to more weight on the drivers and to a 240 lb. boiler pressure compared to the 210 lb. pressure of the R-1. The herald has not yet been repainted on the R-1's tender after a tour through the shops. Heavy modern power was in short supply in 1941 and with the wheat and apple harvest beginning, the locomotive is needed back in service, quickly. (Casey Adams)

RESPLENDENT IN light olive green and Duco engine black, brand new Class R-2 No. 2055 has just rolled out of the paint shop at Hillyard in 1930 and after a testing and breaking in period will be put into service on the Kalispell Division between Whitefish and Shelby, Montana lugging tonnage over Marias Pass. The 30 locomotives of the R-1 and R-2 class (excepting Baldwin built R-1's 2030-2033) were built in the GN shops at Hillyard in the 1928 to 1930 period and were the biggest locomotives constructed west of the Mississippi River. With a tractive effort of 142,055 lbs., nearly double that of a 2-10-2, they could handle most freights unassisted, even on heavy grades. As prime movers of tonnage on the GN, they were unexcelled and reflected the continual search for bigger and better motive power that dated back to the days of James J. Hill. (Lee Pickett)

A CLASSIC PORTRAIT of standard railroading in the thirties, R-2 No. 2054 roars along the mainline in the Montana Rockies, with a mile long string of boxcars. The monstrous girth of the smokebox dwarfs the double compound air pumps hung on it, and the pilot deck mounted headlight moves slightly from side to side in response to the alternate thrusts of the pistons on the front engine. The rear end crew back in the caboose is getting a good ride at this point with the slack between the cars stretched taut, but if meet orders or a red block stop this big fellow and slack has to be taken to restart, the safety rail mounted down the centerline of the caboose had better be used, for the slack running out, will rumble like distant artillery, and the crew in the caboose will be the end men in a crack the whip game. (Lee Pickett)

WITH A MILE OF TONNAGE tied to her big tank, 2-8-8-2 No. 2043 gets underway again after taking water at Halford, Washington on the way east to Skykomish. Halford (a passing track and water plug) is on the long 1% grade up from Goldbar where helper No. 3238 has been cut in behind the caboose. The Mike has kept the slack bunched while the 2-8-8-2 was taking water, and after whistling off, the huge articulated will pull out the slack with a sound like rolling thunder, while the Mike pushes furiously behind the 97 cars. (W. R. McGee)

THE SCENERY along the banks of the Columbia River below Wenatchee is little changed since this late spring day in 1939—nearly 30 years ago. On the far bank westbound freight No. 401, with 115 cars, a monstrous R-1 2-8-8-2 on the head end throwing a cloud of oil smoke skyward, competes for attention with the roar of the water over the spillways of Rock Island dam. (W. R. McGee)

CROSSING THE COLUMBIA RIVER by the Great Northern is accomplished by trains passing over and through this tremendous bridge located south of Wenatchee. First built in 1892, it was rebuilt in 1925 with a new through truss bridge built right around the existing truss. The deck truss approach span on the east side was strengthened in similar manner, and with the old spans left in place, the entire structure became one bridge upon completion of the work. In heavy continuous use for over 70 years, traffic has never been interrupted. (Phil Kohl)

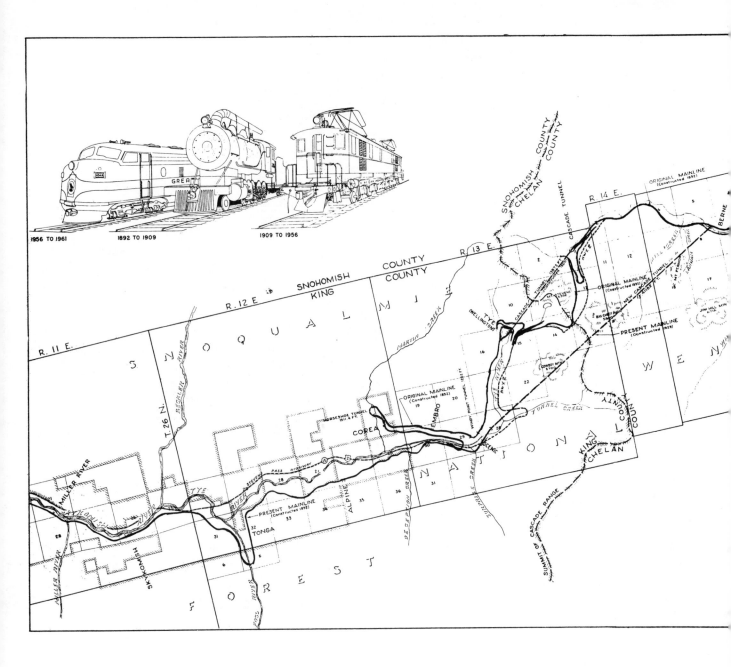

IN THE CLOSING DAYS of steam on the west end of the Cascade Division, Mountain type No. 2521 was assigned to switching chores in Interbay yard. The big modernized 4-8-2, lacking the quick acceleration and stopping characteristics of a yard goat, was completely out of its element and the unhappy experiment lasted only a few days—much to the relief of the switching crews. (Casey Adams)

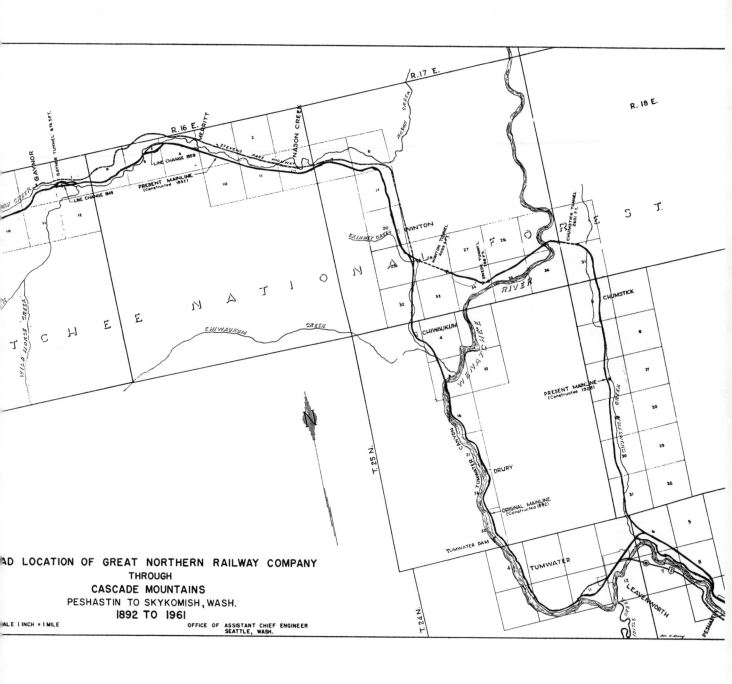

R.17 E.

R. 18 E.

R.16 E.

MERRITT

STEVENS PASS HIGHWAY

NASON CREEK

GAYNOR TUNNEL 674 FT.

LINE CHANGE 1899

PRESENT MAINLINE
(Constructed 1892)

LINE CHANGE 1849

WINTON

WINTON TUNNEL
NASON CREEK

CHUMSTICK TUNNEL
2601 FT.

SKINNEY CREEK

SWEDE TUNNEL

RIVER

CHUMSTICK

WENATCHEE   NATIONAL   FOREST

CHIWAUKUM CREEK

WILD HORSE CREEK

WENATCHEE

CHIWAUKUM

PRESENT MAINLINE
(Constructed 1928)

CHUMSTICK CREEK

TUMWATER CANYON

DRURY

ORIGINAL MAINLINE
(Constructed 1892)

TUMWATER DAM

TUMWATER

LEAVENWORTH

PESHASTIN

T. 25 N.

T. 24 N.

RAILROAD LOCATION OF GREAT NORTHERN RAILWAY COMPANY
THROUGH
CASCADE MOUNTAINS
PESHASTIN TO SKYKOMISH, WASH.
1892 TO 1961

SCALE 1 INCH = 1 MILE

OFFICE OF ASSISTANT CHIEF ENGINEER
SEATTLE, WASH.

ON THE EAST SIDE of Stevens Pass near Winton, Washington during World War II a huge R-1 class 2-8-8-2 has been cut in behind the caboose to add its 142,000 lbs. of tractive effort to the power of the electrics ahead. There is 2% grade between Winton and Berne, and the railroad is struggling with a wartime shortage of motive power. The big steamers haven't been seen in this area for nearly 15 years but the demands of heavy traffic have brought them once again, hot and smoking, up into the pass. (Claude Witt)

EAST OF SHELBY, MONTANA an extra freight with a huge boilered R-2 on the head end works its way east. On this warm October day the fifty cars behind the 2-8-8-2 will not even cause the monster to fluctuate its boiler pressure, but when the temperature drops out in these barren rolling hills and the snow starts flying about Thanksgiving, the oil will stiffen in car journals and the huge articulated will snort and bellow as it forces the dragging tonnage into motion. (W. R. McGee)

WEST OF MINOT, a monstrous R-1 moves heavy tonnage along the mainline, while a gray overcast sky forecasts more snow. Trainlength, in this area, is limited as much by what the drawbars can stand as by the grades. 125 car trains behind one massive R-1 or R-2 were not uncommon, and the slack run out, as a train started, rolled like distant thunder across the prairie, and the vast column of engine smoke could be seen for miles. (Casey Adams)

TIME WAS RUNNING OUT on steam power on the Cascade Division when this photo was taken by Phil Hastings in June, 1951 in the roundhouse at Hillyard. The immaculate condition of both the Mike and the R-1 reflected the pride and the care that the GN took of its power. (Dr. Philip R. Hastings)

S-1 NO. 2550 at Minot, N.D. just off a troop special in the summer of 1941, was one of the six locomotives of the S-1 class which were the first Northerns purchased by the Great Northern from Baldwin Locomotive Works in 1929. They were designed for the 1929 Empire Builder, but in the late thirties and early forties expedited fast freights such as the fruit specials in the Montana Rockies. Low drivered (73″) by comparison with later Northerns such as their S-2 80″ drivered running mates, the S-1's were also about 27 tons heavier. The weight coupled with the lower drivers and slightly larger cylinders gave them considerably more "dig" than the S-2's and a tractive effort of 68,466 lbs. Fitted with the traditional Belpaire firebox, low slung headlight, pump heavy smokebox and large Vanderbilt tank they had the GN look about them. One of the relatively few classes of GN steam engines to be fitted with roller bearings, they were among the last steam engines to be scrapped, probably because of their ability to roll heavy freight at sustained speed. They were in the opinion of many enginemen about the best dual-service locomotive on the GN. (Casey Adams)

FOLLOWING THE TRAIL of the early fur trappers, explorers and missionaries along the Kootenai River near Troy, Montana, S-1 class Northern No. 2551 works its way west with 124 reefers swaying along behind the 48' Vanderbilt tank. The 73" drivered S-1s were fine fast freight engines, more powerful than either the P-2 class Mountains or the S-2 class Northerns and for this reason, were often used in freight service while the lighter faster S-2's held down the passenger and mail assignments. (W. R. McGee)

THE S-2 CLASS NORTHERNS, Baldwin built in 1929/30, were the biggest and most modern steam passenger power on the Great Northern. Originally built with conventional bearings, the 14 locomotives of the class were roller bearing equipped in 1945. This modification, along with the vestibule all weather cabs applied to some of the locomotives, were the only major modifications made up to the time they were scrapped. Long winded engines, fast and durable, their only fault was a tendency to be very slippery when starting a heavy train. The first 4-8-4's to be built with 80" drivers, they had a tractive effort of 58,305 lbs.

The S-2's at times were used in freight service, but using them in this way was like harnessing a high spirited race horse to a lumber wagon. Their forte was passenger and mail service and they are best remembered for their service on the Builder, Oriental Limited and Fast Mail. (Lee Pickett)

WHILE NOT DESIGNED FOR FREIGHT SERVICE, the S-2 could occasionally be found on the point of heavy tonnage. Through the courtesy of W. R. McGee, one of the few photos in existence of an S-2 Northern in freight service, shows No. 2583 leaving Havre, Montana with 2nd #402 an eastbound hot shot. The slippery starting characteristics of the big S-2's was due primarily to their relatively light engine weight of 438,000 lbs. and secondly to the big 80″ drivers. Considerably lighter on the drivers than their 73″ drivered Class S-1 running mates, the S-2's were the first Northerns in the country to be fitted with such a large wheel. Enginemen on the S-2's, much to the consternation of the Master Mechanic often started heavy trains by setting the engine air, pulling out the throttle and then releasing the air. The added kick would urge tonnage into motion without wild slipping, but at the risk of slipping a driver tire and effectively taking the locomotive out of service.

NO. 2585 is feeling a heavy hand from the hogger as the high stepping 80″ drivered Northern comes booming up the 1% grade from the Spokane River Valley towards Hillyard. This Christmas mail extra is running as 2nd Number 4 and only a few signal blocks behind the first section. (Dr. Philip R. Hastings)

TWO MOTORCYCLE OFFICERS in Spokane, Washington pause to exchange small talk with the engineer of 2576 just in from Whitefish, Montana with a westbound Christmas mail extra. This is a quick turn-around run and the mail cars have been moved away by a yard goat. After fueling and fast servicing the Northern will be turned and backed down to an eastbound mail train already being assembled by a switcher. (**Dr. Philip R. Hastings**)

RUNNING AS SECOND NO. 4 a 1950 Christmas mail extra booms up the long 1% grade that takes the railroad out of the Spokane River Valley and into Hillyard. The big Northern on the head end, No. 2585, has a fast wheel on this 10 car extra and the exhaust beat has a steady sustained roar as the green eye of the semaphore signal ahead indicates "Clear!" (Dr. Philip R. Hastings)

HEADING DUE WEST, near Browning, Montana, train number 1, the Empire Builder, has almost reached the highest point (5,213') of the mainline. Since early morning the Builder has been beating its way up the long 1% grade that stretches back almost 150 miles to Havre. The wind is still sharp and the snow has disappeared only recently from these barren brown hills for this is early April and the higher Rockies ahead of the train still wear a heavy mantle of white. By May the hills will turn green briefly and then return to brown again under the baking of the summer sun. (W. R. McGee)

THE HIGHEST ELEVATION reached by the Great Northern is 5,213 feet, at Summit station in Marias Pass. With only 55 miles of the entire mainland above 4,000', the Great Northern has the lowest crossing of the Montana Rockies of the three Northwest transcontinental railroads. With helper districts concentrated in Marias Pass and in the Cascades the GN has been able to confine helper power to a few strategic locations such as Whitefish, Shelby, Wenatchee and Skykomish. This has been a profitable advantage to the railroad through the years and now in the days of multiple unit diesels, freights are dispatched with sufficient head end power to practically eliminate helpers. This is bordering on the miraculous, particularly in the Cascades. In the days of the old mainline up through Tye, three and four engines including Mallets would push, pull and struggle with a 1,600 ton freight at a speed of 5 to 6 mph. (Great Northern Railway)

EASING TO A STOP at King Street Station in Seattle, the Empire Builder has completed another 2,200 mile trip that started at Union Station in Chicago two days and three nights before. On an adjacent track the North Coast Limited, that had arrived minutes before the Builder, waits for a switcher to move in behind the observation and pull the entire consist over to the Holgate street coach yards for servicing. Alongside the Builder's head end cars, the caboose of a northbound freight is slowly easing past, moving towards the south portal of the tunnel under the city. Still the western terminus of the GN and NP transcontinentals, King Street Station is busy in the early morning hours. (Stuart B. Hertz)

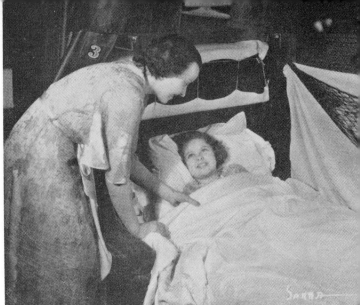

ALL REGULARLY ASSIGNED PULLMANS on the Empire Builder had open sections ranging from the first class 6 section 6 bedroom cars to the 16 section tourist sleepers popular in the West before World War II. Open sections, covered at night by numbered green baize curtains, were the subject of jokes and vandeville humor that outlasted the cars themselves. Actually, the sections at night were more comfortable than they were by day. Even the upper berth was a welcome sight to a tired traveller provided he could go through the necessary contortions of undressing in one of them. The lower berth was the real prize however for here it was possible to lie in bed with the lights out, pull up the window shade and watch the countryside roll by. (Great Northern Railway)

HERE SHOWN is a typical interior of a Pullman assigned to the 1929 edition of the Empire Builder. At night, the carpeted aisle and heavy green baize curtains muffle the click of the wheels on the rail joints, and far off one strains to hear the engine working or the whistle calling for the grade crossings. Comfortable, quiet and stable, they rode like ponderous battleships on their six wheeled trucks. Built to last, with periodic shoppings and overhaul, the big heavy all steel Pullmans probably could have lasted another twenty years, but in 1947 they were replaced with lightweight streamlined equipment. (Great Northern Railway)

THE PULLMANS assigned to the Empire Builder were all named after men who in some way were instrumental in the building of the Great Northern. These heavyweight Pullmans were beautifully maintained during their entire service on the GN even during the full occupancy days of World War II. (Great Northern Railway)

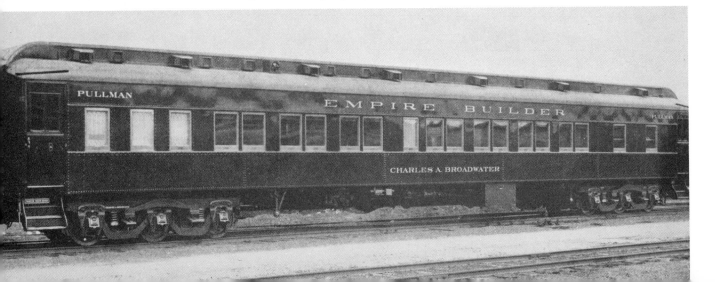

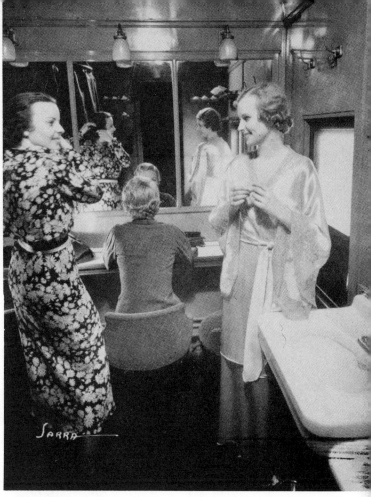

DRESSING LOUNGES for men and women were located at opposite ends of the Pullmans, and their layout was similar except for the dressing table in the women's lounge. The men's lounge on most trains doubled as an informal smoker and gathering place. Being located at the end of the car there was more sway and bounce from irregularities in the roadbed and on fast track it took no small amount of skill to shave with an open razor. (Great Northern Railway)

THE EMPIRE BUILDER was one of the first transcontinentals to use such equipment as the Solarium Lounge observation car James J. Hill, one of seven such cars named for builders of the Great Northern. Not as handsome as the traditional open platform observation car with its brass railing, it was more practical. The sunroom that replaced the rear platform was useable in any kind of weather, and also it was possible, through the addition of an accordian type diaphragm to operate the car in mid-train. (Great Northern Railway)

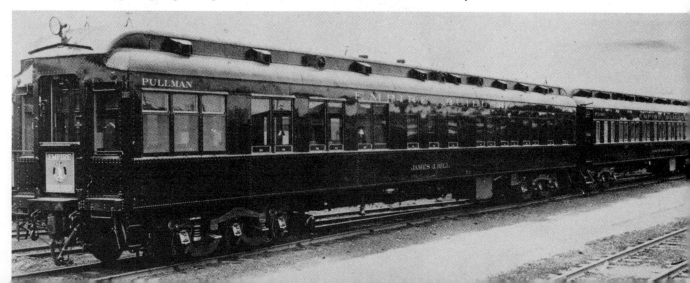

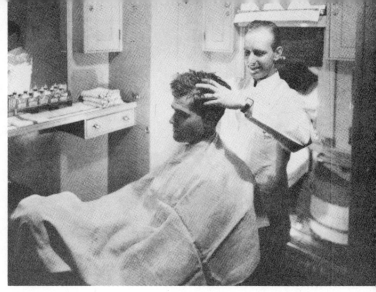

ACCOMPANYING PHOTOGRAPHS show the interior, from the valet's barber shop to the refreshment and observation sections. This car brought the 1929 Tudor decor of the east, to the west, and when the Empire Builder was streamlined in 1947, the new observation cars brought the more informal ranch style decor of the west to the east. (Great Northern Railway)

IN A PICTURE reminiscent of those sold by postcard companies or given away by the railroads during the age of steam W. R. McGee, NP conductor from Livingston, Montana, has caught the Empire Builder crossing the North Fork of the Flathead River near Citadel, Montana on its way west. In this wild, remote country the rugged magnificent scenery dwarfs the railroad like a child's toy and continues for several hundred miles following the Flathead, Kootenai, Pend Oreille and Little Spokane Rivers.

THE ENGINEER AND FIREMAN of a long boilered and vestibule cabbed S-2 class Northern receive running orders in Minot. Magnificent 80″ spoked drivers will start revolving when the conductor waves "highball," and the distinct sharp exhaust of the engine will rattle window panes in buildings close to the track. As the cars slip by ever faster in response to the powerful surges of the locomotive, the wooden platform will echo the sound of the rolling Pullman wheels. (Casey Adams)

ABOUT 25 MILES WEST of Shelby, Montana in a setting about as bleak as can be found on the mainline, the ten car westbound Empire Builder with Northern No. 2588 on the point crosses the long steel bridge over Cut Bank Creek, and sets the steel trusses to vibrating and drumming in response to the tramp of the big drivers and the 1,000 ton train weight. (W. R. McGee)

IN MAY 1949 S-2 NORTHERN TYPE at Ephrata, Washington is shown with the 5 car Cascadian, Seattle-Spokane day train. The big 4-8-4 has been bumped from its assignment on the Empire Builder by diesels, and is now reduced to secondary assignments and protection power status out of Spokane. (Charles R. Wood)

THE BRUTE POWER APPEARANCE of modern GN built steam power is typified by Mikado No. 3388, one of the O-8 class built at Hillyard. The most powerful Mike ever built, rated at 75,900 lbs. tractive effort (without a booster), the O-8's were also the fastest of the GN freight engines thanks to the 69″ drivers and roller bearings. Some of the class were built with all weather cabs and utilized boilers from scrapped 2-6-8-0's. Others were equipped with conventional cabs and were essentially rebuilt Class O-7 Mikados. Three of the engines (3397, 3398, 3399) were constructed in 1931/32 while the remaining 22 engines were built in the early 1940's. (Great Northern Railway)

N-3 CLASS 2-8-8-0 No. 2024, one of 25 similar locomotives, was about the most modern articulated locomotive on the Great Northern roster. Built by Baldwin in 1912 as a compound Mallet, the entire class was simpled during 1925/27. Then in 1940/41 a further modernization, at a cost of 3½ million dollars, provided the class with new nickel steel boilers and appliances and semi-streamlined the cabs by slanting the front edges forward. At this time too, the engines received roller bearings on the drivers, the only class of GN articulateds so equipped. The GN owned only two articulated freight engines equipped with either a four wheel leading or trailing truck, and in fact, over half of the modern articulated fleet (M-2 and N-3 class) had no trailing trucks of any description. The policy of the motive power department seemed to be to put all weight possible on the drivers for maximum tractive effort. The tractive effort of the N-3's was second only to the R-1/R-2 class and was rated at just over 104,000 lbs. Although the articulateds were never seriously considered as dual service engines, during the war, the N-3's were often used on troop trains. Mr. J. S. Miller, Assistant to the Superintendent of Motive Power in 1945/46, has commented the N-3's in troop train service "could run like a deer" at speeds of 50 to 60 mph—most unusual for an articulated freight engine without a trailing truck or four wheel lead truck. (Great Northern Railway)

WITH 97 CARS (6,165 tons) tied to its big Vanderbilt tank, 0-8 class Mike No. 3393 shakes the ground as it rumbles out of Harlem, Montana after stopping for water in September 1952. Biggest and most powerful Mike in the country, the 0-8's were in the estimation of many railroaders, the finest freight power on the GN. (W. R. McGee)

A MODERNIZED N-3 CLASS 2-8-8-0 pants softly in the yard at Minot in the fall of 1941 awaiting the conductor's highball. No. 2006 is on the head end of a 125 car westbound freight mostly composed of empty boxcars destined for wheat loading, further west. (Casey Adams)

SURPRISING, BUT TRUE as far as can be determined from old division reports the most powerful of the articulateds the R-1 and R-2 class 2-8-8-2's never turned a wheel on the heaviest tonnage division of the GN, the Mesabi Iron Range. The Mesabi Division, though, was the stamping ground of almost half the N-3 class 2-8-8-0's. Amazing engines, they hauled ore on the iron range, hustled time freights on the Kalispell Division and served in heavy duty passenger service on troop trains. The GN thought enough of their capabilities to completely rebuild them in 1925/27 and again in 1940/41. Here No. 2024, thirty years old when this picture was taken by W. R. McGee in October 1941, highballs through Cloquet, Minnesota on the head end of 175 empty ore cars headed for the iron range, after unloading earlier at the GN ore dock at Allouez on Lake Superior.

ACTIVE STEAM POWER in the center of this general view of the engine terminal servicing area at Hillyard in February 1951 are SP&S Challengers No. 900 and 910, while stored for use in the event of a sudden unexpected traffic rush are a GN 2-10-2 and 4-6-2. Also visible here at Hillyard are at least three diesel combinations plus a diesel switcher. The rapidity with which diesels took over on the Cascade Division surprised many railfans and some railroad personnel, as practically overight, freights, passenger and mailtrains were locking couplers with multiple F units on the mainline and branches, and steam power was conspicuous by its absence. (Dr. Philip R. Hastings)

PROBABLY THE MOST UNUSUAL ARTICULATEDS on the Great Northern were a pair of Alco built Class Z Challengers, Numbers 4000 and 4001. Built originally for the Spokane Portland & Seattle Railway, a GN-NP owned subsidiary, from the Northern Pacific Z-6 design, they were never popular with the GN and were resold by early 1950, although nearly 600 steam engines were still in service as of this date.

There may be several reasons for the limited acceptance of the Challengers on the GN. They were fine modern locomotives, but the GN took great pride in operating locomotives of its own design and erection. More important, the GN undoubtedly had made the decision some years before the Challengers were resold to dieselize the entire railroad as quickly as delivery could be made. Compared to FT units steam was expensive power to operate and it was good business if steam engines could be resold at a fair price and more diesels could be acquired. Finally the performance of the Challengers operating on The Oregon Trunk line between Wishram, Washington and Bend, Oregon showed no significant improvement over the elderly 1925 Baldwin R-1's which actually were considerably more powerful on the heavy grades with a rated tractive effort of 129,622 lbs. as compared to the 104,500 lbs. of the Z-6. Speed over this line was nearly impossible due to the timecard restrictions of 20, 25 and 30 mph. Under these circumstances the faster Challenger was greatly handicapped and had to operate under virtually drag service conditions.

The Challenger had an advantage in the use of roller bearings that eliminated hot driving boxes, and its increased tender capacity eliminated stops at water plugs that the R-1 didn't dare run by. In the 151.5 mile run from Wishram to Bend the R-1's had to stop four times to take on water and once for oil, while the Z-6's stopped only twice for water.

A series of four tests, under controlled conditions, were made on The Oregon Trunk in September, 1945 by Mr. J. S. Miller, Assistant to the Superintendent of Motive Power, using GN engine No. 2031, an R-1, and SP&S engine No. 905 a Z-6. Both engines handle test trains of around 3,500 tons and their running time over the district (not including water stops) averaged out at 19 miles per hour. The conclusions drawn from these tests were that the R-1's could use roller bearings on the drivers and larger tenders, and would benefit from better maintenance at Wishram where boilers were being washed with cold water—not a recommended practice. In any event the performance of the two quite different locomotives was so similar that any further investment in Challengers, at least on this district was not justified. The story of Challengers on the GN might have been different if they had been used on the mainline through Montana and North Dakota, but heavy freight in these areas was already moving behind four unit diesels and the dynamometer car comparison would have been even more detrimental to modern steam power. (Wally Swanson)

THIS CLASS S-2 ENGINE, built by Baldwin in 1930 and the sole survivor of the last steam engines acquired by Great Northern for main-line passenger service, was placed on permanent exhibition at Havre, Montana on May 15, 1964. (Public Relations Department, Great Northern Railway)

ON A SUMMER DAY in the 1940's the eastbound Cascadian slips downgrade on the east side of Stevens Pass where the trackside rock formations rival some of the rockwork found in Colorado on the narrow gauge Denver & Rio Grande. The single electric on the head end was standard power for the (usual) 5 car Cascadian. Further downgrade, beyond Winton, the regenerative braking will be cut out, and the big motor will whip the consist around the long curves and tangents at a steady 50 mph. (Stuart B. Hertz)

ELECTRICS AND THE CASCADE TUNNELS

Electric operation on the Great Northern began in 1909 with the electrification of the two and a half mile Cascade Tunnel between Wellington on the west side and Cascade Tunnel Station on the east side of the summit of Stevens Pass. This was probably one of the shortest stretches of mainline electrification in the world and in its entirety couldn't have been much over six miles in length, excluding sidings and service tracks. The electrification was vital in the original 2½ mile long Cascade Tunnel, as it was later in the 8 mile tunnel, because of the stiff 1.7% ruling grade eastbound. In the close confines of the tunnel, the smoke and gas from the stacks of steam engines, working hard upgrade, had no place to escape and made working conditions intolerable. The crews were in constant danger of being overcome by the heat and fumes. Gas masks were carried on the locomotives for protection of the crews but there was no way to similarly protect passengers back in the coaches and sleepers. A stalled train, with its crew overcome by fumes, was always a possibility, and would result in asphyxiation for all on board. Electrification was therefore necessary and construction of the unusual three phase system (two trolley wires and the rail for conductors) was completed in July 1909. The four General Electric built locomotives, #5000 to 5003, were undistinguished and even odd looking little box cabs with their two parallel trolley poles in running position and even odder was the fact that their 375 rpm motors allowed a road speed of only about 15 mph. Train tonnage was limited because any tonnage much in excess of 1,600 tons showed the synchronous speed of the motors, with the possibility of motor damage. The steam road engine remained, coupled on the head end of the train for the trip through the tunnel, working just enough steam to prevent dragging. At Cascade Tunnel Station or Wellington the electrics were cut off and steam continued to handle the train the rest of the way downgrade to either Leavenworth on the east side or Skykomish on the west. Actually, then, the electrics were cast in the role of helpers over this short section of the line while steam was still cast in the lead role.

It must have occurred to management, many times, how much simpler the entire operation would be if either the electrics were completely eliminated (impossible with the technology of 1909) or the electric operation was more extensive to eliminate some of the duplication of motive power (and crews).

In the 1920's as freight trains became longer and heavier two or three little B-B electrics simply didn't have enough muscle to pull these longer trains through the tunnel nor was the output of the power plant at Leavenworth sufficient to enable the simultaneous use of the four motors necessary to pull a 2,500 ton train through the tunnel. It was necessary to cut freights in two and in effect "double the hill", a slow, costly and inefficient operation. Electrical engineers though, devised a traction motor connection that enabled the motors to run at just half of their usual 15 mph speed, or 7.5 mph, and draw less current in so doing. This "Cascade connection" as it was known worked very well and four motors now could be used on a heavy freight, two pulling ahead of the steam engine and two pushing behind the caboose, without overloading the power station and freights could go through the tunnel in one piece. Using this connection the B-B motors continued to be used up on the old line until 1927 when the new GE built class Y and Baldwin-Westinghouse class Z motors began arriving from the builders.

In 1925 the GN had made the decision that the old line up through Tye (Wellington) had to go because the operation was simply too difficult, slow and hazardous during the wintertime and maintenance costs were excessive on the snowsheds and old tunnels. Contracts were awarded to the Guthrie Company of St. Paul for construction of the new 8 mile tunnel as well as 19.37 miles of new mainline down the Chumstick Canyon into Leavenworth. As an integral part of this new construction it was also decided to electrify the entire railroad between Skykomish and Wenatchee. During construction of the new tunnel a temporary catenary was erected from Scenic (west portal of the new tunnel where the old mainline doubled back across the Tye Valley to begin its climb up to Tye) to Tye. From Skykomish to Scenic, from Wenatchee up to Berne (just outside the east portal) and through the new tunnel, the catenary was of permanent construction. The old mainline from Cascade Tunnel Station to Leavenworth, which for about half the distance followed the Tumwater Canyon from Skinney Creek to Leavenworth, continued in use as the new main was being constructed further east, across a ridge in the mountains, along Chumstick Creek. The old section of mainline through Tumwater Canyon was not temporarily electrified and steam continued to operate from Cascade Tunnel Station to Wenatchee until several months before the new tunnel was opened in January 1929. In late 1928 the electrification was complete on the new Chumstick line (also called Chumstick cut-off) up to Berne, and although the new tunnel would not open until January, electrics went into operation between Wenatchee and Berne. Between Berne and Cascade Tunnel Station there was a 4½ mile gap in the catenary and steam was used to pull westbound trains across this gap. Eastbound trains operated in a similar manner, either picking up the steam locomotives at Tye or leaving the steam cut in behind the electrics all the way up from Skykomish. This dual operation of steam and electric power between Wenatchee and Skykomish gave valuable experience to the "hill crews" who would be handling the new power over this mountain sub-division. Further, the class Y and Z motors underwent an extensive testing and break-in period before the full responsibility of handling the trains would be turned over to them. Some minor difficulties did crop up, particularly in the braking systems, and these were corrected before any major problems, in service, were encountered.

In January 1929 the new 8 mile tunnel officially opened and with its opening the electrics became "King of the Mountain." While the thundering exhausts and cascading columns of smoke from the steam engines was gone from the high North Cascades the new electrics presented their own show. During periods of heavy snowfall or icing conditions, snow and ice would accumulate on the 11,000 volt overhead catenary to lay undisturbed until the pickup shoes of the locomotive pantagraphs would come sliding along the wire. Then, as the shoes alternately solidly contacted the wire or skipped on the ice ridges the intermittent contact would sputter and arc in a continuing series of brilliant clear blue flashes. At night, the path of a train could be traced for miles as the flashes lit the sky and reflected off the snow, while the headlight peered around the curves, disappearing and reappearing in and out of the cuts.

The new electrics, although practically noiseless compared to steam power, would hum and growl as they worked a heavy train upgrade, and once over the summit, with regenerative braking cut in, would whine coming downgrade like huge streetcars. The regenerative braking system added a second form of control that was similar to having low gears to control the train, as well as the air brakes, and was welcomed by the crews and management as well. No longer was there the risk of dropping down 2% grades with several thousand tons of freight pushing against the locomotive that there was in descending with air brakes alone where a frozen brake pipe could mean disaster. Regenerative braking had been used on the old B-B electrics of 1909 but these locomotives only handled the trains through the old tunnel and were never, of course, used on the steeply curved 2.2% beyond Tye.

While not as spectacular to watch as the steam power the electrics had a distinguished appearance all of their own. The Class Z Baldwin-Westinghouse motors were rather short and stumpy in appearance but operated as two semi-permanently coupled locomotives, not unlike the first FT diesels in an A & B combination did. The Class Y General Electric motors were longer, could operate singly and looked more like big locomotives. The GE motors were also a little faster and usually handled the passenger assignments as well as doubling in freight service. Both locomotive types were painted a conservative olive green and were decorated with imitation gold heralds and numbers. Later, the gold

THE TRACK LAYOUTS in both Wellington and Cascade Tunnel Station yards were relatively simple and served the basic purpose of changing steam to electric power and vice versa. The overhead catenary on the other hand, due to the weight and complexity of the components was quite sophisticated for a six mile long electrification system. In both yards at about 1,000' intervals, heavy steel anchor bridges were installed to support the catenary. Shown here under one of the anchor bridges in Wellington yard are the four (two pairs) motors that were the entire electric locomotive roster of the 1909 three phase electrification. (Great Northern Railway)

lettering was changed to white and the herald to red and white while the carbodies remained olive green.

Through twenty years of service, until 1947, the original order of thirteen GE and Baldwin electrics was not supplemented with new locomotives. In 1947 though, GE delivered two new locomotives, the 735,000 pound Class W's, #5018 and 5019. These were indeed monsters, over 100' long, nearly 16' high (with pantagraphs lowered) the class W's had a B-D-D-B wheel arrangement that equalled the 4-8-8-4 wheel arrangement of the Union Pacific "Big Boys," but, went even further, in that all axles, including the lead trucks, were powered. Their 6,000 horsepower rated them as the most powerful single cab electrics ever built.

The 15 electric locomotives of the Great Northern in service during the post World War II era represented the peak of electric locomotive development and operation on the road. The Great Northern had extensively surveyed the comparative costs involved in continuing or even extending the electric opera-

tion into Everett (or at least as far as Goldbar where the 1% grade started) and in modifying the eight mile long Cascade Tunnel with ventilating fans so that slow-moving freight diesels could operate upgrade through the tunnel. The decision was made to ventilate the tunnel, and with its successful completion in 1956 the diesels could operate between St. Paul and Seattle without power change. The electric operation was abandoned, the catenary came down, the locomotives were scrapped or sold and diesels took over the operation of the 71 mile sub-division between Skykomish and Wenatchee, Washington.

In retrospect, the electrics did a fine job for the Great Northern. For over a quarter of a century they were the prime movers on the toughest division to operate on the entire road. However, like the steam power that they pushed to one side, the electrics in turn, were pushed aside by more modern power that carried their own generating plants with them—the diesels.

THE THREE PHASE SYSTEM OF ELECTRIFICATION, installed in 1909, while satisfactory in most respects was not without attendant problems. Locomotive pick-up trolleys crossing the numerous insulating gaps located above switches in the yards, caused trains to break in two on numerous occasions when the rear motor in a 2 unit locomotive momentarily lost power while the trolley wheels were negotiating the frog pans and insulating gaps in the wire. For a time Class L Mallets were used as pushers to get the trains smoothly out of the yard and into the tunnel. The two overhead trolley wires were normally spaced 5' apart, but in the Cascade Tunnel they were spaced 8' apart, at the insistence of the railroad, so that a brakeman could walk the tops of the cars setting hand brakes if necessary, without danger of contacting one of the trolley wires. This unequal spacing of the wire between the yards and the tunnel was the primary reason the electric locomotives (motors) used the more flexible trolley type collectors rather than bow type pantagraphs. By and large the trolley wheel type pick-up was successful, but on occasion it caused trouble as the wheels jumped the wire and tore down catenary supports. At one time the railroad seriously considered electrifying the 57 miles of mainline from Leavenworth to Skykomish using the three phase system. Problems in the operation of the unusual system however, delayed this until the construction of the single phase system in 1927. (Great Northern Railway)

SNOW that gave the GN so much trouble up on the old Tye line is seen in this photograph. A group of railroad and construction company officials pose during one of the first trips of the new electrics between Skykomish and Cascade Tunnel Station. It is snowing while this picture is being taken and the wet sticky flakes cling to nearly every horizontal surface including the catenary wire and the grab irons on the locomotive. It is not very cold—probably just about freezing—and the water laden snow compacts like deep slush only to slip and slide without provocation. Snowfalls of many feet in a few hours are common and every ridge and rock outcropping holds tons of snow in precarious balance. Little wonder the 25 million dollar Cascade Tunnel has been called the best investment the GN ever made. (Great Northern Railway)

POPPING OUT of the east portal of the old 2½ mile long Cascade tunnel between Wellington (later re-named Tye by the GN) and Cascade Tunnel Station, a trio of the first electrics used in the Cascades, whine up to summit. Limited to two running speeds, 7.5 mph with a heavy freight, or 15 mph with passenger trains, the boxy little electrics built by GE served in this area for nearly twenty years. (Great Northern Railway)

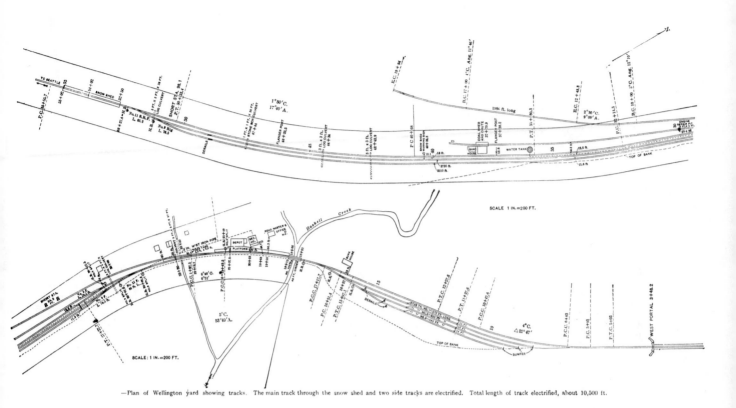

SCALE 1 IN.=200 FT.

—Plan of Wellington yard showing tracks. The main track through the snow shed and two side tracks are electrified. Total length of track electrified, about 10,500 ft.

SCALE 1 IN.=200 FT.

—Plan of Cascade yard, showing tracks. The main track and two side tracks are electrified; the main track to station 42+00. Total length of track electrified, about 8,500 ft

Labels within image:
TUNNEL 2⅔ MI.

MILL
CREEK
SHAFT

NEW CASCADE TUNNEL 8 MILES

WEST
PORTAL

PIONEER TUNNEL FOR CONSTRUCTION PURPOSES

EA
PO

Cascade Tunnel

Tye — CASCADE TUNNEL

Nason

G. N. R'Y.

Mill cr.

Tye — River

NEW CASCADE TUNNEL

Bern

To Seattle — Scenic

MILL CREEK
SHAFT

A DRAWING of the overall layout of the new Cascade Tunnel shows utilization of the unique method of drilling two tunnels side by side in order that construction of the main tunnel could proceed from many working faces rather than from the usual two faces. Main tunnel headings were started from side rooms angling out from the previously drilled Pioneer Tunnel. Pioneer was also used to bring in and out material that would otherwise jam the usual two headings or working faces. That this method of construction was successful can be measured by the fact that other tunnels such as the Moffat (6.1 miles long) and the Connaught (5 miles long) required almost double the drilling time per mile that the new Cascade Tunnel required. (*Wenatchee Daily World*)

LOOKING WEST ACROSS NASON CREEK, the east portal of the 8 mile long Cascade Tunnel appears as a dark blotch against the snow covered mountainside. Down the hill, in the foreground, an eastbound drag down from the old tunnel eases by the watertank and a short cut of passenger equipment parked on the siding. This is the winter of 1927 and the opening of the new tunnel is still better than a year away. (Pickett Photo Co. courtesy GN Rwy.)

DUMP CARS FROM THE TUNNEL, pushed by little electric "mules," are being spotted along the fill at Scenic that is now so high the old water tower is almost hidden from sight. The gap in the fill by the hotel has been left in order that trains can duck under the gap and continue on the old mainline curving back across the valley. On the other side of the valley immediately across from Scenic, the railroad, largely hidden from sight by the snowsheds, resembles the burrowing and tunneling of a giant mole. Looking down the valley of the Tye river towards Skykomish the snowsheds seen through the trees gradually disappear from sight going towards the lower trestle at Martins Creek. Above this point the railroad reappears climbing back towards Scenic several hundred feet higher now. The need for the snowsheds is obvious in the photo. The avalanche area is clearly visible as scars running down the side of the mountain. (Lee Pickett)

AT MILL CREEK, directly over the axis of Cascade Tunnel, a third construction camp was built so that a shaft could be sunk 622′ down to the working level of the Pioneer Tunnel. By this method the tunnel could be attacked from more working faces and the completion deadline of the winter of 1928/29 met.

The Cascade Tunnel between east and west portals actually passes beneath three mountains; Cowboy, Big Chief and Mt. Fennow. Mill Creek is located between the latter two and comes the closest to the tunnel bore of any location between the portals. (Lee Pickett)

BEFORE CONSTRUCTION of the Cascade Tunnel could commence in 1926, several huge camps for the construction workers and engineers of A. Guthrie & Company were built at Berne, Scenic and at Mill Creek high up in the mountains over the tunnel site. These camps were complete with quarters, hospitals, shops, mess halls, commissaries and offices. The camps were of wooden and tarpaper construction not unlike temporary Army barracks or logging camps. For three years these camps were a beehive of activity with work going on around the clock (at one time nearly two thousand men were at work underground), and on payday the little towns of Index, Skykomish and Leavenworth as well as the hotel at Scenic Hot Springs (till it was buried by the new grade) boomed with men in search of entertainment and activity. (Lee Pickett)

WORK WENT ON AROUND THE CLOCK during the building of Cascade Tunnel. A part of the large number of men employed underground are shown in this Pickett photo, as one shift comes out and another prepares to go in. (Great Northern Railway)

THE RAPIDITY with which work on the tunnel progressed is dramatically illustrated in the accompanying two photographs. The upper photo shows the almost primitive beginnings at the west portal in June of 1926. The drilling of the Pioneer Tunnel has recently commenced and the construction site resembles a scene out of the late 1880's. The lower photograph shows the same construction site, just four months later, in October 1926 and already the forms are being built for the west portal of the main tunnel. (Lee Pickett)

A BRACE OF BALDWIN-WESTINGHOUSE CLASS Z MOTORS, 5004 and 5005, pose for their photograph next to the new power house at Skykomish during the winter of 1927. As can be seen by the condition of the running gear—still shiny black—these are brand spanking new locomotives. The class Z motors were usually operated in pairs, or in even more powerful combinations, not unlike the way diesels today are run as multiple units. Two motors running as one locomotive developed slightly over 88,000 lbs. of tractive effort at 15 mph, top speed was about 45 mph. While the class Z's were designed for either passenger or freight operation they excelled in freight service.

In later years heavy beam shaped multiple unit connectors were added to the roofs, over the cabs, of both the class Z and Y motors to simplify the necessary hookup when additional motors were added. Through 30 years of operation the motors were basically unchanged and continued in service right up to the time the electrification was scrapped in 1956.

Their color scheme, when new, was almost identical to passenger equipment of the late 1920's. The carbodies were painted a dark olive green while the herald and numbering was imitation gold. Underbody and running gear was black. Some of the class Y motors were painted in streamliner colors (Pullman green and Omaha orange) after 1947 but no evidence has appeared to indicate this was done to any of the class Z motors. (Lee Pickett)

IN THIS 1928 PHOTO the west approach grade to the Cascade Tunnel is taking shape between the old mainline and the temporary transport line to the tunnel workings. Work proceeded rapidly, and just a year after this photo was taken the tunnel and the new mainline were put into service. (Lee Pickett)

IN THIS 1927 SCENE in front of the hotel at Scenic a pile-driver is building a temporary trestle that will be used to build a fill for the approach to the new Cascade Tunnel. Upon completion of the trestle the work trains from the tunnel will ease out on it and begin dumping conglomerate from the tunnel digging. The new grade is about 32' higher than the old main line at this point but the fill will extend and taper several thousand feet down the valley to keep the grade at 2.2% on practically tangent track.

Scenic Hot Springs had been a popular spa in this area for many years but now it was to be demolished by the new grade, along with the water tower and station, just visible in the far right of the photo. The pony truss bridge will be salvaged along with the rail and other hardware. (Lee Pickett)

WORLD RECORDS for tunnel drilling were established, and then broken, time after time, in the intense rivalry between drilling crews at the east and west portals. Here at Berne camp, outside the east portal, the GN pennant is being raised in honor of the tunnel crew at Berne who drilled a 984' 10 × 10 tunnel in 31 days. The entire tunnel was completed in a record 3 years and 47 days. (Great Northern Railway)

EAST PORTAL OF THE GN RY NEW 8 MILE TUNNEL BERNE WASH 7-2-27 A GUTHRIE & CO CONT.

SIMULTANEOUS WITH WORK progressing from many working faces deep inside the mountain, construction was moving forward outside the east portal. Hard by the east portal flowed Nason Creek which had its headwaters high in the snowfields above the tunnel. Mill Creek joined Nason Creek not far from the east portal and their combined water volume, low in July, during the spring could become a fast moving torrent as it was fed by the melting snow. For this reason the temporary trestlework over the creek, just beyond the portal, will be replaced by a heavy deck girder steel bridge with massive concrete footings and abutments.

Also visible in the photo are four methods of transportation used in the construction of the tunnel. To the right, next to the portal, is a tiny 0-4-0 steam type locomotive. Directly over the locomotive, at the base of the rock slide, is an automobile covered with canvas to protect it from the clouds of dust raised by dumping rock and dirt. In the foreground is a horse drawn wagon used for hauling lumber, and in the center of the photo is the narrow gauge electric construction railroad.

Building the tunnel was a race against time. Due to the deteriorating condition of the snowsheds "up on the hill" the tunnel had to be completed during the winter of 1928/29, and the contractor, A. Guthrie Company of St. Paul, Minnesota, established many world records for drilling speed to accomplish this remarkable feat, including one record of 984' in 31 days. Previously the drilling record (932' in 31 days) had been held by the Canadian Pacific when Rogers Pass tunnel was being constructed in the Canadian Rockies. (Lee Pickett)

THE MEETING AT THE BREAK THRU.
CONGRATULATIONS CAPT. C. G. JONES SUPT. AT EAST PORTAL. & FRANK J. KANE SUPT. AT MILL CREEK SHAFT.

HUNDREDS OF FEET under the mountain and better than 3 miles in from the nearest portal, Captain C. G. Jones and Supt. Frank J. Kane shake hands after the breakthrough in Pioneer Tunnel. Once the Pioneer Tunnel was completed, the work on the main tunnel, directly alongside, proceeded rapidly because the rock could be attacked from many working faces through connecting galleries, a method of construction so much faster than the conventional method of working from only two faces simultaneously that many records for tunnel construction were established. (Great Northern Railway)

SNOW IN THE CASCADES plagued the mainline of the Great Northern and fouled the contractors construction lines running in and out of the Cascade Tunnel. Shown here is one of the unusual little double rotaries that worked on the construction railroad. The snow was shoved to the sides of the wedge plow, picked up by the little whirling rotary blades on each side and then spewed out over the bank. (Great Northern Railway)

THE SUMMIT OF STEVENS PASS HIGHWAY, now U.S. #2 is not far from the Cascade Tunnel although the highway summit is several hundred feet higher than the 2,883' elevation of the railroad summit. Snow remains a continuing problem on the Stevens Pass highway and for miles it is exposed to slides and avalanches from the steep mountainsides that parallel the highway. In this 1927 scene, the spectacular beauty of the high snow covered ridges and slopes give no hint of the sudden crushing blanket of white that slips down inundating everything in its path. (Great Northern Railway)

IN THIS 1928 SCENE two class Z motors and a 3300 class Mikado lead an eastbound freight into Tye, while a pair of class Y motors wait in the siding track. With the tunnel entrance only about a half mile ahead the Mike will soon stop working steam and the electrics will provide all the pulling power through the 2.6 mile tunnel. Once in the yard at Cascade Tunnel Station the electrics will be cut off to return to Skykomish or wait for a westbound train. (Lee Pickett)

IN EARLY 1927 the Baldwin-Westinghouse class Z motors began arriving in the Cascades from the builders. Almost immediately, they were put into service between Skykomish and Cascade Tunnel Station. Here in the small yards at Cascade Tunnel Station, just outside the east portal of the old tunnel, motor #5006 poses with her crew for an official portrait. (Great Northern Railway)

LOOKING LIKE A HEAVY DUTY INTERURBAN the observation car of the Oriental Limited heels to a sharp curve on the old line up to Tye in this 1928 scene. In 1924 the GN updated the Oriental Limited with new Pullman built equipment including seven new compartment observation cars all named in the "Great" series. These cars were the last open observation cars built for the GN and among the first observations to be built with higher windows for better viewing and lighting in the observation end of the car. As train speeds gradually increased the open platform was becoming more dangerous to passengers and further lacked the capability of mid-train operation. Clearances in snowsheds, tunnels and station platforms was tight in many cases and an unwary or foolhardy passenger could be injured when hanging out beyond the sides of the car. Observation equipment that followed, known as solarium-observation cars, were entirely enclosed. (Lee Pickett)

IN MARCH of 1927 the new catenary was complete from Skykomish to Tye, and existing catenary from Tye through the old tunnel was modified as a single phase system. To provide additional needed power a new power house was erected at Skykomish and the old power house at Leavenworth continued in service, now operating as a single phase system. The interior of the Skykomish power house is shown in this photograph along with one of the 7,500 kilowatt single phase machines. (Great Northern Railway)

IN 1926/27 THE GREAT NORTHERN extended electrification of the mainline from Tye (Wellington) down the 21 miles of 2.2% to the little railroad town of Skykomish. The electrics would now lift the 2,500 ton trains up to as well as over the summit of Stevens Pass. Gone now was the sound and fury of steam wrestling with the long grade up through Scenic, Martins Creek and around Windy Point as it pulled, pushed and hauled the trains up among the high peaks of the North Cascades. In its place were the nearly silent electrics that started and accelerated a heavy train with a low humming noise and moved easily around the sharp curves like flowing water. From tall poles catenary arms extended over the rails from which the trolley wire was hung and the skeleton like pantagraphs on top of the locomotives reached for the wire with thin steel fingers. In the winter season pantagraphs sliding along the trolley wire would arc and sputter like a welder's torch, as accumulations of ice and snow were burned off, and the blue flashes could be seen for miles in the deep winter night, as they marked the progress of a train winding along the sides of a mountain. (Lee Pickett)

IN THIS 1928 SCENE one of the new GE built electrics #5010 leads a P2 class 4-8-2 into Skykomish on the head end of a passenger run. Entering service late in 1927 they were operated from Wenatchee and Skykomish both as helpers and road engines to familiarize engine crews with their operation and to work out any bugs inherent in their design or construction before the new tunnel opened in 1929, and the entire sub-division from Wenatchee to Skykomish would be exclusively in the hands of electric power. Once the new tunnel was opened, and the old route through Tye abandoned, it would be impossible to work a steam engine through it going upgrade from west to east. On occasion steam power did go through the new tunnel, but only as a drifting engine, not working steam.

Skykomish itself retained its status as a crew and engine change point, and the town through the years has always been very closely identified with the railroad. Here viewed is "Main Street" where every building faced the railroad, and across the tracks various railroad structures including the new transformer facility beside the water tower. The raw barren look is emphasized by the logged and burned over mountainsides just beyond the town limits. This destruction and waste in logging was widely practiced in the "old west." Fortunately, in recent years, these scarred mountains have been covered once again by second growth timber. Logging is now more selective, and fire prevention practices are strictly enforced by law. (Lee Pickett)

A 3 UNIT HOOK UP of class Z motors is shown in the yard at Skykomish before moving out to take another drag over the hill to Wenatchee. With a combined tractive effort of 132,000 pounds the three motors were as powerful as one of the monstrous R-2 articulateds and under a short term overload rating were even more powerful. On 5,000 ton freights the power was balanced between the head end and mid-train, three units on the front and two or three in the middle was typical. This procedure helped to equalize the strain on drawbars as well as to prevent any tendency to pull over cars in the middle of the train when rounding, or starting on a sharp curve. (Lee Pickett)

AT CASCADE TUNNEL STATION a long westbound freight hangs just over the summit while Mike #3353 steams softly—its helper chores done for this day. Retainers are being set up by the train crew for the problem now is easing the tonnage down to Tye and thence down the 21 miles of 2.2% to Skykomish, in many ways a more difficult task than getting the train up to the summit. (Lee Pickett)

CASCADE TUNNEL STATION was located a few thousand feet outside the east portal of the old tunnel, next to the passing and storage tracks used when the B-B electrics were cut into or out of the trains passing through the tunnel. Along with the little hamlet of Tye barely 3 miles west, on the other side of the tunnel, there was only one reason for its existence—the railroad. Like Tye, Cascade Tunnel Station was practically inundated by snow during the winter months and it was a continual battle keeping the snow dug, plowed, and pushed out of the way so that operations could continue. There were few regrets when it was abandoned upon completion of the 8 mile tunnel. (Claude Witt)

THE ORIENTAL LIMITED whines upgrade across Foss River Bridge, in the summer of 1927, behind a pair of class Z motors and a P2 class Mountain type. (Lee Pickett)

IN LATE 1927 construction of the new Chumstick cut-off was progressing rapidly in spite of the large amount of heavy fill and rock work needed. At camp 15 one of the longer fills was being built of earth and rock excavated from the deep cuts. Note the temporary trestlework and how the fill is being gradually built up to rail level, thereby covering completely the spindly trestlework that is just heavy enough to support a work train. After a period of settling and shaking down, the fill will become as solid as the rest of the roadbed on either side. (Lee Pickett)

JUST OUTSIDE one of the snowsheds in the Tumwater Canyon a rail gang is picking up rail from the old roadbed in July 1929. The Wenatchee River flows through Tumwater Canyon on its way down to the Columbia and the swift running stream caused the railroad more than a few headaches in time of high water during the spring run-off. Through much of this area U.S. Highway #2 is built right over the old railroad right of way. (Lee Pickett)

LEAVENWORTH, WASHINGTON was for many years a division point of the Great Northern between Seattle and Spokane. When the railroad was electrified from Wenatchee to Skykomish the division point was moved to Wenatchee about 22 miles further east on the Columbia River. The old yards, roundhouse and even the mainline was torn up and a new main was constructed on the other side of town for direct access to the new Chumstick cut-off. In this early 1929 photo, the new grade, station and catenary are shown through Leavenworth. (Lee Pickett)

WHILE THE CASCADE TUNNEL was being built, work was going on simultaneously in the Chumstick cut-off, building a new grade down to Leavenworth that would eliminate much of the curvature and troublesome slide areas in the Tumwater Canyon along the Wenatchee River. In this photo, temporary construction track has been laid to allow the A. Guthrie Company saddle tank locomotives to get the blasted rock that will be used as fill and rip-rap further down the line (Great Northern Railway)

POUNDING UP THE NEW GRADE in the Chumstick cut-off a 2500 series Mountain type leads a passenger run in the last days of steam operation before the electrics took over. The wan winter sun and soft shadows serve to disguise the raw harshness of the new grade while the billowing canopy of engine smoke blots out most of the background. The big steamer is working hard up this long tangent grade and the roaring exhaust echoes and re-echoes among the high ridges and cuts. (Lee Pickett)

THE "HIGH CAR" used in maintaining the catenary through the old tunnel was also used during construction of the new tunnel and its electrification system. Later, it was stored at Skykomish for many years and has finally disappeared from the equipment records. In this 1928 scene it is slowly moving past the station at Scenic, with its crew of railway electricians en route to some other spot on the line where its retractable high platform is needed. (Lee Pickett)

A DRAG FREIGHT powers its way upgrade over Lower Martin Creek trestle in 1928, just before entering Horseshoe Tunnel on the near end of the bridge. In the tunnel, the motors will start curving in the opposite direction and once out of the tunnel, and across the upper trestle, will appear on the line just above the trestle headed the opposite way. If the freight is a long one, the conductor in the caboose will be able to look above and behind him to see the motors approaching the upper snowsheds. Such twisting and contorting of the mainline was necessary to keep the grade anywhere near 2%. While the North Cascades are not particularly high mountains (most peaks range from 6,000 to 7,000') they are very steep and change abruptly, without the benefit of high valleys and wide canyons, for the rails to follow on a more gradual and direct ascent.

The snowsheds in the picture had been lengthened and strengthened every year since the line was opened in 1893 in an effort to keep railblocking slides at a minimum and prevent tie-ups that lasted as long as ten days. These sheds were stoutly built of 12×12 and 12×24 timbers. The roof section was additionally strengthened with half inch steel sheathing. Their annual maintenance ran into the hundreds of thousands of dollars. Even so, many were deteriorating rapidly when this photo was taken. Elimination of these sheds—about nine miles of them—was one of the major reasons for construction of the new tunnel. (Lee Pickett)

CLASS Y MOTOR #5016 waits in the yard at Skykomish for an eastbound passenger train, probably the Cascadian. The GE built class Y's were quite a bit larger than the Baldwin-Westinghouse class Z's, and operating as a single unit developed 60,000 pounds of tractive effort—about equal to a 4-8-4 Northern type. Their top speed of about 50 miles an hour was all that was necessary in mountainous territory. Behind the motor is coupled one of the little 30′ train heating cars used in passenger service because train heat boilers were not built into the carbody of the electrics, as first delivered. (Lee Pickett)

NEW YEARS DAY 1929, twelve days before the official opening of the Cascade Tunnel, a ballast train moves up to the west portal. The track is receiving final adjusting as is evident by the quantity of track working tools just inside the entrance and outside, partially hidden by fresh snow, are the odds and ends of new construction. (Lee Pickett)

AS WORK ON THE NEW CASCADE TUNNEL was being completed and finishing details applied, it was used at times by construction and gravel ballasting trains, such as this one posing for the photographer, Lee Pickett, in the center of the tunnel. It is a long walk in either direction (nearly 4 miles) to a portal and the confines of the tunnel are extremely tight if a train should come through at the same time. Refuge bays, located every 2,000 feet through the tunnel, provided for such contingencies but it was (and is) strictly forbidden to enter the tunnel without prior approval and supervision of railroad officials.

NEW GE ELECTRIC #5012 leads an eastbound passenger train, for the last time up through the snowsheds coming into Tye. The miles of prime quality timber, comprising millions of board feet of 12×12 and 12×24 beams and braces that went into these sheds was fantastically expensive to maintain. Crews worked on these sheds every summer and early fall preparing them for the tons and tons of pressure the snow would exert on their roof and side structure during the winter months. Inside the sheds on the embankment side log cribbing or concrete walls held the earth and rock back from the rails. On the outer edge, more log cribbing and concrete or rock retaining walls were used to brace the roadbed. Some sheds, like those just west of Tye were nearly solid concrete construction. Without them though, operation over this line strung along the mountainsides was impossible. (Lee Pickett)

SIMPLE ARTICULATED 2043, R-1 CLASS 2-8-8-2, has picked up the last eastbound train over the old line at Cascade Tunnel Station for the 4.5 mile trip across the non-electrified section. In a few hours the new tunnel will be opened to traffic and the railroad from Wenatchee to Skykomish will be in the capable hands of the new electrics, as they air born their way past Cashmere, Dryden and Leavenworth pulling thousands of tons of merchandise behind their abbreviated snowplow pilots. (Lee Pickett)

RECORDED FOR POSTERITY by Lee Pickett the first train through the new tunnel (from east to west) pops into foggy daylight at Scenic behind a pair of Baldwin-Westinghouse motors. The fireman assumes a Casey Jones pose expected of an officially photographed crew member in the 20's and 30's. While not noted on the photograph, this could well be another ballast train working on the new section of mainline, as the two units on the head end are rather light power for the 5,000 ton freights that immediately started using the line. (Lee Pickett)

THE OPENING OF THE NEW TUNNEL in January 1929 drastically changed operation across the summit of the Cascade Division from that of a convoluted and steeply graded mainline requiring hours to cross under the most favorable conditions to a truly heavy duty mainline with broad sweeping curves, and a rifle bore tunnel permitting 5,000 ton freights to cross the summit in an hour. The grades were still fairly stiff in a few places (up to 2.2%) but with the new motors such as B 5006 leading 104 loads (5001 tons) up the grade from Merritt to Berne on the east side of the Cascades, available in quantity, trains were no longer limited to 2,500 tons. (Lee Pickett)

1929 WAS A BIG YEAR FOR THE GREAT NORTHERN with the opening of the new Cascade Tunnel and inauguration of the transcontinental Empire Builder, then in September The Cascadian, named for the scenic beauty of the mountains it crossed, was placed in service between Seattle and Spokane. With 25 scheduled stops and numerous conditional stops along its 330 mile route, The Cascadian was not a particularly fast train, but it filled a need for a daylight train between Seattle and Spokane. It is difficult in 1967 to recall the poor condition of U.S. Highway #2 that paralleled this route or the near impossibility of getting across Stevens Pass in the winter. The train was the most comfortable and (even at an average of 30 mph) the fastest way to make the trip.

A typical consist of the Cascadian included a baggage car, mail car, two coaches and the Cafe-Observation carrying the rear markers. At times, when head end business was light, the baggage car was not used. The photo by Lee Pickett shows such a consist at Berne station just beyond the east portal of Cascade Tunnel, probably taken in the late spring of 1930. From the arms akimbo stance of the conductor standing between the tracks one might conclude that he is not too pleased with the delay while the picture is being taken.

MOTOR #603, formerly of the Spokane, Coeur D'Alene & Palouse Interurban Line, has been modified for use on the mainline during construction of the Cascade Tunnel. The little "juice jack" has received new bow type pantographs and the internal wiring has been modified to accept the 11,000 volts pressure from the catenary. Several of these little motors were used for several years pulling construction trains and work equipment. Later, they were sold to Seattle City Light and used at Ross Dam on the Skagit River. (Lee Pickett)

JUST OUTSIDE THE REPAIR SHOPS at Appleyard a brace of class Z motors await servicing. The engine numbers 5002-A and 5002-B indicate that this is one locomotive composed of two units, a numbering practice confined to the class Z motors and similar to the numbering used on the first diesels that also operated as multiple units. (Casey Adams)

AN ABBREVIATED ORIENTAL LIMITED rumbles across the steel bridge over Surprise Creek just outside the west portal of Cascade Tunnel in the spring of 1929. This is probably one of the press or inspection trains the GN ran just after the new tunnel was opened because it includes neither the diner nor sleepers, and also because the Oriental Limited on its regular schedule passed through here at night, not during the day. (Lee Pickett)

IN ONE OF THE BETTER KNOWN promotional photos of the new 1929 Empire Builder some remarkable enthusiasm is shown for both the new solarium-observation car and the surrounding country by the passengers looking through the rear windows of the observation car as it enters the east portal of Cascade Tunnel. There is little doubt that the scenery up through Chumstick Canyon and across the summit of the Cascades, thence down along the banks of the Tye, Skykomish and Snohomish Rivers is some of the finest in the Northwest, but assuming that the Builder is running on time and will be in Seattle at 9 A.M., up here at Berne, Washington (105 miles from Seattle), it is only 5 A.M. (Lee Pickett)

ONE OF THE REASONS GREAT NORTHERN electric locomotives were in superb running condition after nearly 30 years of continuous heavy service, was the extensive repair and maintenance facility at Appleyard. In this well lighted and fully equipped shop the locomotives received the best maintenance and servicing that the railroad could provide. When several of the class Y motors were sold to the Pennsylvania Railroad after electric operation on the GN had been terminated, some Pennsylvania officials expressed doubt over the condition of the conventional brass bearings on the running gear. Examination showed however that axle bearing assemblies of the class Y's were as good as the day they were built. This was not surprising in view of the fact the GN has always been known as "a good housekeeper." (Great Northern Railway)

POSED OUTSIDE THE SHOPS AND ROUNDHOUSE at Appleyard are 5019, the most powerful single unit locomotive on the GN, 416 a four unit FT freighter and one of the massive homebuilt R-2 class 2-8-8-2's. Both the FT and the R-2 saw service on the Cascade Division during World War II when the electrics had more tonnage than they could handle and Chumstick Canyon once more reverberated to the sound of a roaring steam exhaust as the big R-2's shouldered in behind the tonnage freights. The steam engines were used as pushers, cutting off on the fly before the tunnel portal was reached, while the electrics and diesels continued on through. Being used as the buffer between the engine and the tonnage does not contribute to a serene and smooth ride up a mountain grade and more than one conductor and rear end brakeman said a prayer as the pilot on the huge steamer pushed mightily behind the caboose while it tried to do a tango along the rails in response to the moves and lunges of the engine. (Great Northern Railway)

"HIGH CAR" X 838, a converted diesel powered railcar of uncertain ancestry, replaced the old single truck high car soon after the opening of the new tunnel in 1929. Used for inspection and maintenance work on the overhead catenary it was not electric powered as the rear pantagraph would seem to indicate. The pantagraph was raised, along with the retractable work platform, whenever work was being done on the wire. The pantagraph served to ground the car and protect the electricians working on the 11,000 volt line. (Walt Mendenhall)

HIGH UP ON FOSS RIVER BRIDGE, during World War II, four class Z motors are cut into an eastbound freight as midtrain helpers. Foss River Bridge on the west side of the Cascades between Skykomish and Scenic, closely resembles the Martin Creek trestles on the old mainline, and shares the distinction with them of being built on a ten degree curve and a grade. Speed restrictions are always in force on this bridge due to the curvature. The unfortunate #5011 took its tumble on the east approach to this bridge as a result of excessive speed.

During the war the electrics on the Cascade Division did yeoman service. There simply wasn't time to service them as regularly or as carefully as is usually done in GN shops and yet they were kept running day and night between Skykomish and Wenatchee with freights, passenger, mail and troop trains. Their record of service was amazing for locomotives that were built in 1927 and 1928, particularly so in view of the fact that both the class Y and Z motors were built with conventional brassed journals rather than roller bearings. Even so, the times that locomotives of either of the classes were out of service due to bad bearings was practically negligible. When the Pennsylvania railroad purchased some of the class Y motors after the electrification was scrapped in 1956, they were amazed at the excellent condition of the units that required nothing more than modification to Pennsy standards to go right back into heavy pusher service. (Stuart B. Hertz)

THE GENERAL OPERATING RULE of "going in the hole" for the varnish does not necessarily hold true in territory where heavy grades are involved because of the difficulty, delay, and expense incurred in restarting a tonnage freight upgrade. Under these circumstances the dispatcher will usually order the passenger train (varnish) into the siding (hole) and let the freight (drag) continue to power its way upgrade without pause. The Cascadian (Seattle-Spokane local) shown here has taken the siding in deference to the tonnage somewhere around Dryden or Cashmere, Washington just to the west of Wenatchee.

This photo was taken during World War II when any equipment that operated to the coast was under blackout or dim out restrictions. The unusual looking markers on the Cascadian's observation car are standard Adlake lamps with sheet metal hoods over the lenses to make them less visible at night, conforming to the restrictions. The electrics of course did not come within miles of Puget Sound and therefore the headlight or class lamps are not hooded.

The Cascadian was the only pasenger train to traverse Cascade Tunnel during the daylight hours. The schedule put the eastbound Cascadian through the tunnel just past noon, while the westbound slipped into the east portal about a quarter to four in the afternoon. GN timetables of the thirties carried this footnote, "The temperature in the Cascade Tunnel remains about 60 degrees throughout the year—the observation platform may be used in any season." While the 11 hour schedule between Spokane and Seattle offered little inducement to passengers, the attraction of the tunnel did and the Cascadian to the end of World War II was well patronized. (Stuart B. Hertz)

EARLY IN 1940 the traffic on the GN (as on many western roads) began to grow under the pressure of an economy geared for defense production and the requirements of lend-lease. Westbound traffic from the middle-west was considerably heavier than eastbound traffic—a pattern unchanged appreciably since the railroad was first completed. Manufactured goods, heavy machinery and Orient bound merchandise moved west while lumber, fish, fruit, imported merchandise and some light manufactured goods moved east.

In the Chumstick Canyon about 3 miles west of the old division point at Leavenworth, in May 1941, a trio of class Y electrics are on the point of 122 cars (5,000 tons) westbound for the coast. The grade is 1.6% stiffening to 2.2% as the line climbs towards Cascade Tunnel. Back about 70 cars a trio of class Z motors push and pull for all they are worth as the long freight hangs down the grade and around the broad curves. The total tractive effort of the 6 motors working this train is about 314,000 lbs. with a speed of around 15 mph. The motors are producing a deep steady hum indicating they are working at very near capacity.

Trains such as this would have been impossible in the days of the old line up through Tye. Now, however, the days of "maximum ton miles, minimum train miles" has arrived and the railroad with its heavy duty mainline and low profile from Minneapolis/St. Paul through to the coast is operating as Jim Hill envisioned it would a half century ago. (W. R. McGee)

ACCIDENTS of a serious nature on the electrified section of the Cascade Division were few and far between. The completion of the new tunnel in 1929 along with new stretches of track and new equipment largely eliminated the old operating hazards. During World War II however the westbound Fast Mail, train #27, was the principal in one of the most spectacular flips ever taken by an electric powered GN train. Coming downgrade in the dark early morning hours and carrying a load of high priority military equipment in the head end cars, #27 got as far west as the approach to Foss River Bridge. Here, at high speed, it left the rails and plunged down the steep embankment into the trees and brush below. There was no visible damage to either the rails or right of way as the photo at the accident scene testifies. There were fatalities among the train crew and head end personnel and damage to equipment was severe. Motor #5011 was so badly damaged the carbody was scrapped but the frame and running gear were salvaged. A new streamlined carbody was built by the GN shops utilizing 2 FT diesel nose sections, and #5011 was put back into service, unique as the only streamlined class Y type in service. (Claude Witt)

WRECKAGE of mail and express cars line the bottom of the embankment behind #5011. Out of the 8 or 9 cars involved in the accident only one was salvaged. (Claude Witt)

SMASHED BEYOND REPAIR, electric #5011 lies at the foot of the approach embankment to Foss River Bridge. The carbody was lifted out of this location and scrapped while the running gear was salvaged and put into service again under a home built carbody complete with streamlined diesel nose sections. (Claude Witt)

#5011 lays at the bottom of the Foss River east embankment with the wreckage of a mail car twisted around it. Only the air horn in the near foreground on top of the 5011 identifies the carbody of the motor. (Claude Witt)

THE CARBODY OF #5011 is lashed to two flatcars at Skykomish after being pulled up the railroad embankment at Foss River. Part of the truck frames that were salvaged and put back into service under a new carbody, are visible on the track behind the first flatcar. (Claude Witt)

#5011, A CLASS Y ELECTRIC built by GE in 1929 is on the point of the Empire Builder at Skykomish in the summer of 1948. The streamlined appearance of #5011 is due to an extensive rebuild of the carbody by the Great Northern shops, after the locomotive took a spectacular spill off the east approach to Foss River Bridge during World War II. The running gear and frame was salvaged after the carbody was twisted and smashed beyond repair. #5011 after its rebuilding was often mistaken for one of the huge class W's delivered in 1947. Actually, the locomotives were completely different in appearance, but the streamlining common to both types, caused the confusion in identification. (Walt Mendenhall)

REBUILT #5011 class Y electric is ready to pull out of Skykomish coupled to a pair of E-7 passenger diesels. The big motor has been extensively altered in appearance by the addition of a pair of diesel nose sections purchased from General Motors in the early 40's. Between the cab doors a new carbody has been built by the GN shops to fit around and over the electrical gear, and the familiar Omaha orange and Pullman green color scheme of the new diesels adopted. Often used as a helper on the E-7 powered Empire Builder or as road engine on the Cascadian, the big motor was unique on the Cascade Division and the object of much curiosity by those not familiar with its history. (Walt Mendenhall)

A PAIR OF CLASS Y ELECTRICS await their next assignment with folded pantagraphs in the yard at Skykomish. Little changed through the years—even to their old cross barred windows—the motors are still in fine condition due to careful maintenance and overhaul procedures at the shops in Wenatchee. The only apparent changes since their delivery out of the erecting shops at Erie, Pennsylvania are their streamliner color scheme and the heavy bus bar type multiple unit connection over the cab that is stenciled "Danger 11,000 volts," necessitating lowering of the headlight to a position in front of the cab door. (Casey Adams)

#5018 (one of two GE built 5,000 hp electrics) designed for heavy mountain service, emerges from the west portal of Cascade Tunnel during a lull in a snowstorm. The huge class W's were slightly over 101' long and rode on 16 drivers with a four wheel lead truck at each end. The lead trucks were unusual for they not only helped guide the huge locomotive, but also shared the work, since all axles were fitted with traction motors. Unlike the class Y and Z motors, the Class W's were fitted with roller bearings on all axles. Like the older motors the class W's were equipped for either passenger or freight service, but were not designed for multiple unit operation and were usually seen on the head end of freights with helpers cut in far back in the train. The GN, like the Southern Pacific, believed in mid-train helpers while frowning on pusher engines. Mid-train helpers, while more difficult to cut in and out of a train at helper stations, balanced the power better producing smoother operation with less wear and tear on equipment. During World War II, when the availability of electric and diesel power reached the critical stage, some steam pushers were used, up to the Cascade Tunnel portals. Here they cut off on the fly and the electrics and/or diesels continued on the easier grade in the tunnel. This was a wartime expedient however and was not repeated once electric and diesel power was readily available again. (Great Northern Railway)

FOSS RIVER BRIDGE located east of Skykomish, Washington on the west slope of the Cascades is one of the more spectacular structures along the mainline. Built of timber in 1892 it was rebuilt with steel in 1901 and strengthened several times after that. Located on a series of compound curves that range from six to ten degrees the bridge carries a speed restriction of 20 mph. In this photo a Bridge & Building gang is replacing one of the steel supporting struts during the winter of 1964/65. (Claude Witt)

HIGH UP IN THE CASCADES, #5018 rolls across a deck girder bridge, with a drag freight in tow. The huge locomotive, with its powered lead truck swinging out from under the carbody on the curve of the bridge, weighs over 735,000 lbs. Heavy as a "Big Boy" (without tender) and with the same 4-8-8-4 wheel arrangement it was classified as a B-D-D-B type. (Stuart B. Hertz)

AN IDEA of the tremendous size of the class W's, compared to the older electrics, may be gained in this photo by Walt Mendenhall at Sky. The high cab of the 5018 looks across the top of the class Z and some engineers and firemen instinctively ducked when approaching tunnels for the first time, certain the huge locomotive would never fit the tunnel bore. Clearances in tunnels were snug in any event and big motors fitted the tunnel like wadding going down a rifle barrel. (Walt Mendenhall)

LOOKING LIKE A SQUARE EYED MONSTER with a headlight for a nose and with the gap between pilot and carbody forming the mouth, #5010 breaks trail through new snow east of Skykomish, not long before the electrification was scrapped in 1956. The snowplow pilot on #5010 can handle accumulations of snow about a foot deep, but if these big sticky flakes continue to fall heavily sterner measures will have to be taken.

While the North Cascades are not plagued with the deep sub zero temperatures found in the Dakotas and along the Canadian border, they are noted for vast accumulations of snow with a high water content that sticks like white glue and packs into icy masses when tackled by a rotary plow. In the days before the new tunnel was opened, the mountains often reverberated with blasts of dynamite needed to clear the drifts and slides or at least reduce the depth to the point where rotaries could handle them. Closing of the line due to snow is practically unheard of now although delays are encountered and some scuffing of paint occurs when bucking through a small slide. (Casey Adams)

THE DIESELS

The Great Northern was the first road in the Northwest to utilize diesel power, when in 1926, the "oil-electric" No. 5100, 600 hp. switcher, joint product of Alco, Ingersoll-Rand and G.E. was purchased for use in the Minneapolis/St. Paul terminals, heralding "a new era in railway operation and equipment in the Northwest." Moderately successful, the 5100 continued in active service through World War II, but as early as 1939/40 the Great Northern, along with many other railroads, faced the need for the eventual replacement of an aging steam fleet. The existing power on the road was inadquate to handle the increasing traffic already beginning to move west, and over the iron range in Northern Minnesota, and new, heavier power was needed.

Into this picture in the Spring of 1940, came the Electro Motive Division of General Motors with EMD demonstrator No. 103, the prototype of the famed FT. This four unit 900,000 lb. freight diesel could exert a maximum tractive effort of 228,000 lbs., or better than double the tractive effort of two N-3 class 2-8-8-0's, and on other railroads was showing better than 90% availability, doubling in passenger service as well as freight.

Actual tests on the Great Northern showed what the diesel demonstrator could do. In March of 1940, on the east–west mainline, No. 103 whipped 5,000 ton time freight 402 from Wenatchee to Minneapolis at an average speed of 31 mph, not far off the timecard of the S-2 powered Empire Builder. Up on the iron range, No. 103 took better than 16,000 tons out of Kelly Lake down to the Allouez docks at Superior, and in between times, running as two units, handled both passenger and freight trains between Duluth and St. Paul. Here was a locomotive suitable for any type of road service from passenger to the heaviest freight drags that could be hung on its drawbar. It had nearly all the advantages of the electrics in regard to multiple unit operation, economy in fuel costs, availability and reduced servicing facilities, without the handicap of expensive catenary and sub stations, and without dependence on an outside source of power, the failure of which could paralyze an entire sub-division.

After the remarkable demonstration of 103, the road moved quickly to purchase production FT's, and eventually became the second largest owner of this type in the U.S. with 96 units. In 1939/40 the GN was also taking delivery of a number of EMD switchers, and by 1942 there were 40 units on the roster. During this same period, the GN also took delivery of seven, essentially stretched out switchers, NW3's that were fitted with FT type trucks, a steam generator for passenger and a 1,000 hp. twelve cylinder engine. Ten more of these units, slightly modified, were bought after the war in 1946, making the GN the biggest owner in the country of the predecessor of the GP series.

During World War II a number of the FT freighters were concentrated on the Cascade Division out of Wenatchee, and on the Kalispell Division helping freight and passenger trains up and over Marias Pass. These two points were the toughest sub-divisions to operate with grades of 2.2% and 1.8% respectively, and the FT's kept these potential bottlenecks open and fluid. Without them the GN probably would have been forced to acquire more heavy steam power such as Challengers and Yellowstones. During this period the production and allocation of diesels was under the strict control of the War Production Board, and some railroads which like the GN were sold on the merits of diesel operation, did reluctantly accept delivery of heavy steam power as a stop gap measure.

As far as much of the public was concerned, the Great Northern's first venture into diesel locomotives began in 1947 with the inauguration of the new diesel powered streamlined Empire Builder. This handsome new train, the first passenger train to be delivered to any railroad since 1942, caught the eye and fancy of the traveling public. With the inauguration of the new Builder, the old Oriental Limited was revived, powered with diesels, and equipped with the heavyweight steel cars and 63 hr. schedule of the old Builder.

The new Empire Builder was originally assigned two unit, 4,000 hp. E-7 passenger diesels (delivered in 1945 after the WPB relaxed the ban on building passenger units), but the 112 mph geared E-7's simply could not cope with the demanding 45 hr.

WITH CHARACTERISTIC high pitched whine coming from their blowers, four new GE-U25B's pull by the control tower at Hillyard in the summer of 1964. (Great Northern Railway)

Chicago-Seattle schedule when running in mountainous terrain, with the original twelve car sets of Builder equipment running as high as eighteen cars during the summer months, and with no booster or "B" units that would operate satisfactorily with the E-7 A units, and they were soon replaced by high geared, but more powerful four unit FT's or P3's.

Between 1947 and 1954, as delivery began to catch up with long standing orders, diesels began arriving from the builders in great numbers. GP-7's and GP-9's were delivered by the dozens. SD-7's and SD-9's were delivered for special service that required light axle loadings, and F-7's and upgraded F-3's added new power to the streamliners. Alco delivered road switchers and a few "covered wagons" that eventually found a home on the west end of the Cascade Division and steam power was seen less and less on the railroad. The last unheralded steam run was made in 1958 and the steam engines that had worked on the system for nearly a century were scrapped, a few donated to cities along the line for display.

Today the era of steam is past, and the electrics too have been swept away by an avalanche of diesel power, cooled by a man made gale that blows across their radiators, while climbing the eastbound grade inside Cascade Tunnel. Even the FT freighters, that chanted up the long mountain grades with staggering amounts of wartime tonnage banging along behind, have disappeared from the railroad to be replaced by more powerful and efficient diesels, ranging from the general purpose GP-9's to the SDP-40's on the head end of the Western Star/Fast Mail.

Yet much in railroading remains the same. Mid-train helpers are still common place in the Cascades where speed often drops to a fast walk as the heavy freights grind up the 2.2% with diesel engines howling from the strain and ammeters flickering into the overload ratings. Two Medicine, Gasman Coulee and Columbia river bridges still vibrate from the tramp of the heavy laden cars rolling across them. Out on the prairies, and in the still darkness of the mountain passes headlights pierce the blackness with blinding white beams as the CTC and automatic block signals show their gleaming emerald and red aspects. Inside the lead units engineer and fireman still call "clear block" across the cab in response to the green signals and chime air horns call their warning and greeting at the crossings and stations.

AT CASHMERE, WASHINGTON just to the west of Wenatchee, a four unit freight diesel idles under the old catenary waiting to help a westbound drag over the hump to Skykomish. (Walt Thayer)

A NOTABLE FIRST scored by the GN was the purchase in September, 1926 of the first diesel locomotive to see service in the Northwest. Number 5100 was a joint product of American Locomotive (car body and running gear), Ingersoll-Rand (the 2-300 hp engines), and General Electric (supplier of electrical components), and was designed for service in the Minneapolis/St. Paul terminals. Looking much like some of the smaller electric box cab motors in use at this time, the 5100 was termed by the railroad, an "oil-electric locomotive," since it burned diesel oil in the engines, which in turn powered the generator that supplied current to the traction motors. Moderately successful in the terminal service for which it was designed, the 5100 pioneered diesel operation on the Great Northern. (Casey Adams)

New Oil-Electric Locomotive
First in the Northwest

AN EMD 800 HP SWITCHER stands in the yards at Minot during the early part of World War II. A part of the 1939 order from General Motors, the unit is still painted in the black color scheme, with a huge red & white GN herald decorating the sides of the hood. The barbed wire coils, on the front platform of the locomotive, were intended to discourage any would be saboteurs from climbing on the engine out of sight of the fireman or engineer. It would be interesting to know how many student brakemen of this era, unfamiliar with this obstacle at night, tangled with the barbed wire and thought that war had indeed come to North Dakota! (Casey Adams)

EMD BUILT Class NW-3 1,000 hp. road-switchers, seven of which were delivered to the Great Northern between 1939 and 1942. The switcher style headlight indicates yard duties while the FT type trucks indicate road service. Not visible is the steam generator that made the locomotive suitable for mixed and light passenger service. The Unusual NW-3's were successful enough that the Great Northern purchased 10 more slightly modified versions in 1946, Class NW-5. (Casey Adams)

CLASS NW-5 ROAD SWITCHER was the immediate predecessor of the GP series and as the photo shows is very similar to a GP-7 except for the lower long hood and lack of continuous side handrails. (Casey Adams)

E-7's NO. 501 AND 502, being refueled at Interbay, are painted in the color scheme that was applied when the locomotives entered service in 1945, several years before the introduction of streamlined passenger equipment in 1947. Not as well known as the F units that have powered the Builder and the Western Star during most of their service life, the E-7's have been used on the Internationals and Red River streamliners. Because of their high speed gearing and attendant difficulties in trying to run with F units they haven't been used on the Builder since the late 1940's. (Great Northern Railway)

ON A CLEAR JUNE NIGHT in Spokane the eastbound Empire Builder has switched the cars from Portland, Oregon, via the SP&S, on to the train, and is about ready to depart for the east. Due to the short platforms in the GN's through type station in Spokane, head end equipment and the engine units on this long train are strung out on the bridge across the Spokane River. The westbound Builder is still streaking along the double main outside of Spokane, and in a few minutes, in a flurry of green and orange with lighted windows, a whoosh of air and the sound of hurrying wheels, will pass the eastbound. Then as red and green end markers fade from sight, quiet will return to the Spokane Valley. (Dr. Philip R. Hastings)

AGAINST A BACKDROP of high snowclad peaks in Glacier National Park, the Empire Builder glides over Two Medicine Bridge in the summer of 1948. The Omaha orange and Pullman green with gold striping used on the Builder, after years of somber green and black color schemes in the standard steel heavyweight equipment era was certainly one of the most striking exterior color designs in contemporary railroading. Keying the interior decor to Northwest Ranch Country, and drawing on the culture of the Blackfeet Indians for paintings in the Observation and Ranch cars was a complete change from the earlier Tudor decor, and gave the people of the Northwest "their streamliner." In what was probably one of the fastest replacements of passenger equipment in railroading history the 1947 Empire Builder, shown here, was completely replaced by new equipment for the "Mid-century Empire Builder" in 1951. This included new Pullman dome cars and later a full length "Great Dome" for coach passengers. With the advent of the fast streamlined Builders of 1947 and 1951 (45 hrs. Chicago-Seattle), it was no longer necessary to travel via Portland, Oregon and the Union Pacific to Chicago to enjoy the luxury and speed of modern equipment. (Great Northern Railway)

THE WESTERN STAR in Spokane, June 26, 1951, sets out mail and express cars at the station before proceeding on to Seattle. When the streamlined Builder was put into service in 1947 the old heavy-weight standard steel equipment was renamed the Oriental Limited, and operated on the slower schedule of the old Empire Builder. With delivery of the new equipment in 1951, the Builder's 1947 streamlined equipment replaced the standard steel equipment of the Oriental Limited, and in a "name the train" contest, the Oriental Limited became the Western Star. The Western Star remained on the old Empire Builder 63 hr. Chicago-Seattle schedule which included the seasonal stops at Glacier National Park and the longer routing via Fargo, North Dakota. The Western Star also picked up all the conditional stops and head end work along the line which the Builder didn't have time to make, and like the NP's Mainstreeter became the maid of all work across the Northwest on the GN. The Western Star's Spokane stop is an important one because much head end work is done here, and the Builder's schedule, other than picking up or setting out SP&S connecting cars, doesn't allow time for this. While the Western Star is many hours slower than the Builder between the Twin Cities and Seattle, on the Cascade Division, from Spokane to Seattle their running time is almost identical.

In the general retrenchment of passenger schedules since this photo was taken the Western Star and The Fast Mail now operate as one combined train, with the Western Star/Fast Mail coming into Seattle at night, and the Empire Builder arriving in the morning. (Dr. Philip R. Hastings)

EXTRA 199 SOUTH, on the sixth subdivision to Moscow, Idaho crosses the Spokane River in 1951 over an old wooden bridge dating back to the turn of the century. The Alco road switcher on the head end is running long end forward which was standard operating practice on the GN before the advent of the new low nosed diesels. Early model Alco's like No. 199 made a peculiar burbling sound when idling that made them easily identifiable even when the locomotive was out of sight, and when starting a train they would often emit a large cloud of black smoke that shot into the air somewhat like the exhaust of a steam engine. (Dr. Philip R. Hastings)

TRAIN #28, the combined Western Star/Fast Mail pauses briefly in its hurried flight east at Havre, Montana to take care of some head end work. Number 28's westbound counterpart, #27, often leaves Minneapolis with 22 or 23 cars of mail bound for the west coast, while #28 eastbound often pulls out of Seattle with 14 or 15 cars of mail plus the two coaches, a diner and two Pullmans. (Walt Grecula, GN Rwy.)

MOVING TENS OF THOUSANDS of carloads of wheat during the wheat harvest season, the Great Northern is the principal grain hauler of the Northwest. In 1963 the railroad hauled 3,622,260 tons of wheat, the bulk of it carried in clean but older boxcars which had been spotted along sidings and spurs across North Dakota and about half of Montana before the wheat rush began in late summer. While most of the wheat comes out of North Dakota, an amount equal to about half of the North Dakota carloadings originate at wheat elevators like these "Prairie Skyscrapers" at Dutton, Montana. (Great Northern Railway)

ALONG MARIAS PASS high in the Montana Rockies a trio of GP's push a steam rotary into a huge snowslide that has tied up the dual main of the GN after bulldozers and plow equipped "Cats" have scaled down the depth of the slide to the point where the rotary can move in without being buried in a tunnel of its own making. (Great Northern Railway)

BEYOND THE SOUTHERN BOUNDARY of Glacier National Park, and out onto the Blackfeet Indian Reservation, the Empire Builder of 1957 accelerates after climbing the 1.8% eastbound grade in Marias Pass. With the mountain grades and curves west of the Continental Divide falling behind the observation car, and the long tangents and low hills of Central Montana just ahead, the eastbound Builder will now utilize the 79 mph gearing of the F-7's. (Great Northern Railway)

FROM THE middle of June to the middle of September each year, the Western Star has scheduled stops at Glacier Park station and Belton, Montana the east and west entrances to Glacier National Park. In the days of steam power, the Empire Builder, which then ran on a slower schedule, did the honors, but today's Empire Builder passes both stations with a greeting from the air horns. There simply isn't enough pad in the accelerated schedule to include these stops. A promotional bit that has become traditional is to have authentically costumed Blackfeet Indians meet the train, to the delight of the reservation Indians and the tourists. (Great Northern Railway)

SKIRTING THE SHORE of the Pend Oreille River near Newport, Washington a time freight, with four 2250 hp GP-30's on the head end, hustles eastward toward the Idaho state line, where it will again swing north to pick up the Kootenai River at Bonners Ferry, Idaho for a water course eastward through the Montana Rockies. (Great Northern Railway)

LEANING HARD into the superelevation of the new bridge across the Skykomish River at Index, Washington a westbound freight swings around the long curve and fill that bisects the little mountain town of Index. This new bridge was built in 1963 as part of the multimillion dollar line relocation to eliminate a horseshoe shaped compound ten degree curve that was slowing traffic and limiting tonnage. Known on the railroad as bridge 1764.4 it is unique in the respect that it is a tangent (straight) through truss design located almost in the middle of a 6 degree curve. Like its predecessor, which is now being torn down by a B & B (bridge and building) gang, it is wider than usual to accommodate the continuing curve, but unlike the old bridge, the track through it is superelevated for the highest possible speed. (Chas. R. Pearson photography, courtesy GN Rwy.)

A WESTBOUND FREIGHT with four F units on the point comes whining around the new curve just west of Index, Washington with heavy tonnage strung out behind, around the long curves. Older diesels, not equipped with dynamic braking, come down the hill on the 2.2% above Skykomish under a steady brake pipe reduction to keep the train under control. Wheat drags that are exceptionally heavy for their 60 or 65 car length trains, leave behind a haze of blue brake shoe smoke that fogs the road bed; eastbound freights, traveling the same route some minutes later, can trace the descent of the westbound by the smoke still hanging above the road-bed. (Great Northern Railway)

ALONG THE SHORE of Puget Sound between Seattle and Everett a pair of F3 freighters speed northward with a time freight. The new heavy rock fill termed "the million dollar mile" has been constructed to withstand the scouring action of the tidal currents and large waves that lash the shore in the wintertime, and to move the mainline further out into the sound away from the mud slides that continually come down from the sand and clay bluffs during the rainy weather. (Chas. R. Pearson, courtesy GN Rwy.)

ALONG THE LENGTH of Puget Sound from south of Tacoma to Bellingham on the north, the high speed freights hustle night and day on their way to and from Seattle, Portland, Vancouver, B.C. and the East. At night, the big multiple unit diesels barrel around the bluffs and promontorys leaning into the super elevation on the wide sweeping curves. The gyrating mars lights, on the earlier model F units, light the banks and right of way with a continuous rolling motion, while the lower headlight casts its blinding white beam along the railheads made silvery by heavy use. The high pitched drone of the engines rises and falls, as they accelerate or shift down, for slower or faster sections of track. During the day, the green and orange bands of color on the engines can be seen for several miles, and the passenger trains look like gaily striped ribbons moving around the bluffs. In the photo an eastbound freight rolls into big curve above Golden Gardens recreation area in the north end of Seattle. (Forde Photographers, courtesy GN Rwy.)

TRAIN #358 the northbound International Limited crosses a long rock causeway just south of Bellingham, Washington on its way to Vancouver, B.C. Following the shores of Puget Sound for better than half of the 156 mile distance to Vancouver, the International operates through some of the most beautiful country in the Pacific Northwest, with scenery easily the equal of that between San Francisco and Los Angeles, traversed by the better publicized Coast Daylight streamliners of the Southern Pacific (Stuart B. Hertz)

PULLING A LONG CUT OF CARS up the yard lead at Interbay, a GM built switcher clumps over the frog of a switch as the diesel engine howls in protest at the heavy load. Across the yard tracks and high iron a pair of switchers occupy the roundhouse lead while an idling Alco A unit grumbles to itself with that peculiar distinctive slow idle characteristic of early model Alco engines. (Phil Kohl)

A MIX OF FREIGHT DIESELS idle on the roundhouse ready track, in the fast fading light of a fall evening in Seattle, with an Alco slated to be first out. To the far right, the high iron of the mainline curves between the roundhouse tracks and yard tracks, to the left a block and call on signal controls movement of engines to and from the mainline, and a lunar white signal indicates a spring switch at the entrance to the roundhouse lead track. (Charles R. Wood)

AN ODD LASH-UP of two yard switchers, with an Alco road switcher on the point, is about to clump across the NP crossing in Interbay yard. The switchers are deadheading, possibly to Everett, and will replace two others coming back to the Interbay shops for servicing. (Phil Kohl)

A WESTBOUND MAINLINE FREIGHT, just down from the Cascade mountains to the east of Seattle, whines down the mainline at the north entrance to Interbay yard. The wet snow on the ground in Seattle, is rapidly melting, but the pilot and nose of No. 3025 show evidence of bucking the deeper snow falling in the mountains. (Phil Kohl)

FRESHLY CLEANED, washed and stocked, the eastbound Builder, with every seat in the dome cars occupied, drones under a little wooden bridge in Ballard, after crossing the huge drawbridge across Salmon Bay at the entrance to the Government locks in the ship canal. Running slowly, until all of the following cars have cleared the drawbridge structure, the diesels will begin to growl in earnest as they pull the long and heavy Builder up to a 60 mph cruising speed along the Sound.

By dinnertime the Builder will be in Stevens Pass close to Cascade Tunnel. Dinner is already being prepared in the diner, just ahead of the Great Dome car, and soon passengers will have to decide whether or not to leave the vantage point of the dome and give in to the tantalizing odors coming from the diner. (Charles R. Wood)

JUST CLEARING the north yard limit of Appleyard at Wenatchee, a Geep powered drag freight accelerates along the banks of the mighty Columbia River. Appleyard, named for the lush fruit country in which it is located, is the distribution point of some 18,000 carloads of apples and soft fruit grown in the region. During the late summer, the empty ice reefers are spotted, in anticipation of the coming rush, along every siding and spur clear to the Canadian border, and the Wenatchee-Oroville branch line takes on the look of a refrigerator car storage track. With the advent of the fall harvest, solid trainloads of apples pour in from the branch line, as GN extras pick up the loaded yellow reefers from the apple warehouses. At Appleyard the reefers are blocked into long cuts and dispatched east and west as expedited fruit trains. (Great Northern Railway)

TRAIN #254 the Wenatchee-Oroville local passes a work train "in the hole" at Okanogan, Washington. The caboose of the work train is typical of GN wooden cabooses a decade ago, with the distinctive roof hand rails, bright red paint, striped platform safety shield and "Billy goat" end herald. (Walt Thayer)

DIESEL POWERED Motor Car. No. 2325 pauses at the small station in Chelan, Washington on the Wenatchee-Oroville branch line, in June of 1953. The elderly Brill built car had seating accomodations for 34, a mail compartment, and a baggage compartment. On days when head end business was heavy, a 70' mail storage car or coach trailed the motor car and carried the rear markers. The 137 mile trip (daily except Sunday) took 5½ hours and allowed sufficient time to work the 10 regular stops and 18 conditional stops. Indicative of the major crop of this fruit growing region, two of these stops were the little towns of Stayman and Winesap. After a short turnaround at Oroville, the train worked its way back to Wenatchee via Omak, Okanogan, Riverside, Pateros and Chelan. (Walt Thayer)

EXPRESS MESSENGER Roger Reed performs head end work at Chelan, Washington, while agent Bill King and his dog Lady assist. The Wenatchee-Oroville local, now removed from the timecard, was typical of branch line passenger and accomodation service on the GN that at one time had 30 motor cars bounding over the prairies and hills on the many sub-divisions from Minnesota to Washington. (Walt Thayer)

CONDUCTOR AL BATTLES does his bookwork between stations on train #254 in his "office" in the coach. GN employees timetable #87 is close at hand, while his well worn leather grip, carrying the badge and tools of his trade, occupy the seat across from him. (Walt Thayer)

EASING ACROSS the 1792′ long bridge spanning Gasman Coulee, a westbound freight behind a mix of diesels, including GP-30's, GP-35's and a GE U-25B, has just left Minot and Gavin yard. Most of the cars, in the long freight, still have to negotiate the passing track switch just beyond the semaphores, at the far right of the picture. Once the caboose has cleared the switch, the diesels will begin to wind up, and in a few miles, the train will be up to passenger train speed on the long tangents leading to Williston, North Dakota 120 miles west, and the Mountain Time Zone. (Great Northern Railway)

A WESTBOUND FREIGHT, behind a pair of old FT's, leaves Gavin Yard at Minot, North Dakota. Gavin Yard, the biggest and most modern hump yard on the system, does the lion's share of classification work for the entire railroad. (Great Northern Railway)

THE EMPIRE BUILDER, looking like a toy train running amongst full scale mountains, skirts the boundary of Glacier National Park along the middle fork of the Flathead River in Montana. (Great Northern Railway)

AN EASTBOUND FREIGHT, just down out of the Cascades, drifts downgrade along the Wenatchee River a few miles above its confluence with the mighty Columbia at Wenatchee. (Great Northern Railway)

THE FIR AND PINE COVERED HILLS plunge into the clear blue-green water of the Little Spokane River in Northeast Washington, two thousand miles from the populous east and better than 500 miles from the Pacific. The air is clean and scented with evergreens and warm grasses along this watercourse close to the Canadian border. Thinly populated, it is still a land of deer, bear and a variety of wild life. Devoid of freeways, large cities or heavy industry, it is a country of ranches, sawmills and gravel crowned byways. The stillness is broken by the musical chime horns of the Builder, The Fast Mail, the hard working freight diesels, and the rumbling wheels of the heavy laden cars. (Great Northern Railway)

THE CASCADIAN, Seattle-Spokane daytrain, dawdles along the Skykomish River behind a GP-7 westbound for Seattle. In the days of steam a Pacific would be on the point after the train left Skykomish, but electrification is now a thing of the past (as is steam) and the GP-7 has been on the point since the train left Spokane this morning. The consist of the Cascadian has changed very little since its first run in 1929 and here in 1957 the one concession to modernity is the repainted orange and green coach ahead of the Cafe-observation car. The serviceable, but elderly, equipment includes a mail storage car (second from the engine) that saw service on The Fast Mail during the first World War. One of the few local runs left on the GN in the fifties The Cascadian was removed from the timetable on August 17, 1959. (Great Northern Railway)

THE EMPIRE BUILDER, its swift journey east slowed by the mountain grade and curves, slips by Sunset Falls along the Skykomish River. (Stuart B. Hertz)

ALMOST BURIED by compacted drifted snow a new rotary plow, with four diesels pushing, attacks drifts in North Dakota on the Surrey line in early March of 1966. Blizzards sweeping out of Canada along the mainline in Dakota and Montana still present snow fighting problems of the first magnitude. The drifts pile up higher than car tops in the cuts and draws along the track, and the sub zero cold thickens diesel oil, freezes exposed fingers and ears, takes the breath away in icy blasts and numbs movement as it penetrates the warmest outer garments. (Great Northern Railway)

TWO NEW GENERAL MOTORS SDP-40 3,000 horsepower units team up with an older F-7 A unit on the head end of train #28 the eastbound Western Star/Fast Mail, at King Street Station in Seattle. Scheduled for a 10 P.M. departure, this January 1967 evening #28 is heavy with 12 mail and express cars, two coaches, a diner and two Pullmans cut into the middle of the consist. Formidable appearing with a long rectangular high hood, low notched nose, huge fuel tanks slung between massive 6 wheeled trucks, the new diesels are so powerful that the heavy train often has to brake going into curves on the long grade up to Cascade Tunnel. Looking more like freight than passenger engines, they are appropriate on the mixed consist of #28, and as a brakeman on #28 remarked, "This is the only freight train in the world that has a dining car." (Charles R. Wood)